THE PARABLES OF LINA WERTMÜLLER

Pasqualino (Giancarlo Giannini) after carrying out an execution in *Seven Beauties*.

The Parables of Lina Wertmüller

by
Ernest Ferlita
and
John R. May

PAULIST PRESS
New York/Ramsey/Toronto

Copyright © 1977 by
The Missionary Society
of St. Paul the Apostle
in the State of New York

All rights reserved. No part of this book may be reproduced or transmitted in any form or by any means, electronic or mechanical, including photocopying, recording or by any information storage and retrieval system without permission in writing from the Publisher.

Library of Congress
Catalog Card Number: 77-83562

ISBN: 0-8091-2048-8

Published by Paulist Press
Editorial Office: 1865 Broadway, New York, N.Y. 10023
Business Office: 545 Island Road, Ramsey, N.J. 07446

Printed and bound in the
United States of America

Contents

Introduction: Myth and Parable 1

Part One: The Artist and Her World 7

Part Two: The Parables of Lina Wertmüller 17

   I. Images of World 19

   II. Images of Woman 26

   III. Images of Man 38

Conclusion: An Image of the Future 69

Interview with Lina Wertmüller 76

Appendix A: Works of Lina Wertmüller 88

Appendix B: Reviews of the Films 92

Appendix C: General Bibliography 95

Notes 97

Acknowledgements

The authors wish to express their gratitude for all the help received during the research and writing of this book.

To John Kirvan of Paulist Press for inviting us to do it.

To Alexis Gonzales, F.S.C., to whom this book is dedicated, for helping us gather research material and arranging for our convenience the rental of several Wertmüller films through the Film Buffs Institute of Loyola University in New Orleans.

To Newline Cinema, Cinema 5, New Yorker Films, distributors, who made these films available at a very reasonable fee.

To Maria Landry and Pamela Yarbrough for the careful typing of our manuscript.

To Tonino Benetti who generously provided us with stills for *The Seduction of Mimi, Love and Anarchy, Swept Away,* and *Seven Beauties.*

To Alicia Colombo, secretary to Lina Wertmüller, for supplying us with data.

To John Navone, S.J., for helping one of the authors arrange and conduct an interview with Lina Wertmüller.

And, of course, to Lina Wertmüller herself, who graciously granted the interview.

Our book is itself an expression of thanks for her very special artistry.

To Alexis

pure e disposto a salire a le stelle
—*Purgatorio,* XXXIII, 144

Gennarino (Giancarlo Giannini) and Raffaella (Mariangela Melato) in *Swept Away*.

Introduction
Myth and Parable

Recent scholarship has greatly enhanced our understanding of myth; students of comparative religions and of the history of religion have made notable efforts to save the word from a graveyard of abuse and misunderstanding. In everyday conversation, if one were searching for a word to describe false recollections or groundless opinions about historical characters, it seemed that the word *myth* would almost invariably crop up. How often did we hear, "That's pure myth!" Or in the aftermath of America's recent and horrifying political assassinations, commentators were often quick to assert that it would not be long before the careers of John F. Kennedy and Martin Luther King would take on mythic dimensions, implying that the country, in assuaging its corporate guilt, would distort the truth of these men's lives. Myth-making, where it is functioning properly, may of course distort the *facts* of their lives, but it could never distort the *truth,* for myth in a political context is the imagination's way of preserving the genuine achievement of great men and women. It gives a public dimension to the personal, human truth that builds community.

Myth, in its purest and earliest form, is simply story. It was and is a people's cultural story, their attempt to express in narrative their own self-understanding. The problem has been that most of the best-known myths, at the roots of every religious heritage, are considered by the modern secular mind to be without historical verification. But how can one *verify* self-understanding? What proof is capable of supporting the deepest truth that a people can express about themselves, their understanding of their relationship to the world, to others, and to God? Our modern scientific and historical sophistication was and is, unfortunately, ready to throw out the baby with the bath. Without intellectual strain, however, one can easily distinguish narrative and meaning, the fictitious elements of story from the ultimate reaches of truth. The fact remains that man's richest projections of meaning, in the history of human culture, have always been imbedded in story. Philosophical and religious discourse is the product of a different, and decidedly younger, though questionably better, mode of imagination.

In the Judaeo-Christian tradition, much of our recent insight into the truth of myth has come from an honest confrontation of the dimensions of our oldest cultural stories. Faced with scientific discovery and evolutionary hypothesis, the contemporary believer has learned, for example, to sort out fictive elements from religious truth in the myth of the garden in Genesis. The Yahwist strand of the Genesis narrative presents our primitive religious self-understanding in terms of this ideal: Man and woman were made to live in harmony with nature, with each other, and with God. So the Yahwist tells a story of a man and woman sharing an idyllic existence with God and nature. But this is not all that the story professes. It is designed also, perhaps primarily, to express the belief that humankind alone is to blame for the disruption of harmony. Humanity creates its own punishment; it is not imposed from without. We know, of course, how this fundamental truth of Judaeo-Christianity is given flesh in story in Genesis 3.

This series on "The Mythmakers" is built on the assumption, commonly held by interpreters of contemporary culture, that we are living in a period of transition between the disintegration of the old myths that held our lives together and the expectation of something new. Amos Wilder has called our age's characteristic experience "loss of world."[1] In the volume that initiated this series, Charles Ketcham, commenting on our major film directors, expresses it this way: "All seem to be saying that the old symbols which have structured the lives and thoughts of Western culture are now ineffective and powerless, that we are beginning a new era in which these old symbols must be redefined or in which new symbols must be created or discovered."[2]

Crucial to an appreciation of this cultural rite of passage is an

Introduction: Myth and Parable

understanding of the function story plays in the process. We feel that this is especially pertinent to the subject of this book—Lina Wertmüller's contribution to the search for a new mythology. Aside from the extremes of experimental cinema, our culturally typical films—and hers are no exception—are all visual stories (although other terms are used by critics to designate this element, e.g., *continuity* or *narrative line*). To say that films are stories is not of course to deny that they are primarily visual-aural experiences (aesthetic experiences manifesting technical excellence and philosophical statement, as Ketcham has explained[3]); it *is* to deny that they are to be treated as if one minor aspect of that experience—dialogue, for example—were the major factor to be considered in assessing their meaning. The peculiar context and overall structure of the visual story must be analyzed as a guide to the total meaning of the film. Thus in analyzing Wertmüller's films, it is important, we feel, to know the specific kind of visual story she employs as well as the cultural context it is seen against. Wertmüller's films, we feel, are visual parables; their context will be defined by the dominant assumptions of the popular Italian culture they so clearly satirize.

Parable, according to John Dominic Crossan, is at the opposite pole of story from myth. Myth constructs a world through story, he notes, not just by attempting to mediate the seemingly irreconcilable, but particularly by establishing the very possibility of reconciliation itself. The basic function of myth then is to demonstrate the possibility of solution. Parables, on the other hand, bring not peace but the sword; they are meant to change us, not reassure us. Parables keep us humble by reminding us of limit and in this way prepare us, Crossan suggests, for the experience of transcendence. Parable subverts the world that myth establishes.[4]

Jesus' parables, for example, undercut the popular religious assumptions of his day—pharisaical man's confident claim to understand the true nature of God, man, and the world. Against belief in a God who rewarded according to strict demands of justice, his stories described a world characterized by unexpected favor and bountiful mercy. He told stories of masters and servants, of vineyard keepers and laborers, of treasures hidden in fields. It is interesting to note that in Jesus' parables (except for the rare instances of allegorization by the early Church of the Scriptures) God is never a character, yet no one would deny their profound religious significance; the stories clearly speak of God indirectly, symbolically, contextually.[5] If they are religious primarily because of their context—and this is almost certainly the case—then the religious roots of contemporary culture provide possibly an adequate context for an initial recognition of the religious potential of the best of recent cinema. It is not the way of modern culture either to people stories with gods, yet its stories nonetheless can have profound religious significance.

This book is concerned principally with the films of Lina Wertmüller, their parabolic meaning, their cultural context. However, any discussion of an artist's achievement needs perspective. The first, and by far the shorter part of our work, is devoted to the artist and her world. It is an attempt to sketch a brief portrait of Lina Wertmüller, person and artist. Even her severest critics admit she has achieved a position in the field of film direction and scriptwriting unrivaled by any other woman. In America at least, men have been among the first of her critics to praise her achievement in the medium, to drop the sexist label, and to indicate her developing reputation in relation to the proven masters of the art: "A couple more films like *Seven Beauties*," writes John Simon, "and Lina Wertmüller will take her rightful place among the grand masters of cinema: the Fellinis and Bergmans, the Antonionis and Renoirs."[6] This first part, therefore, explores briefly her artistic background and its influences, her acknowledged range of cultural concerns, and the reaction of her critics.

The second part of this book is devoted exclusively to her films. We have taken as our frame of reference two of the three images customarily associated with cultural story—world and others. And since the dynamics of the sexes is obviously so important, we have treated "others" separately as "images of woman" and "images of man." Although it was necessary under each of these headings to mention at least briefly most if not all of her films, we have given fuller treatment, in each of the sections, to the film or films in which a particular image seemed dominant. Thus, *All Screwed Up,* which seems more concerned with an image of world than with development of character, is analyzed in greater detail in "Images of World." For analogous reasons, the analyses of *Swept Away* and *Love and Anarchy* dominate the section on "Image of Woman," and *Let's Talk About Men, The Seduction of Mimi,* and *Seven Beauties* the section on "Images of Man." The third and final image related to cultural story—the image of the transcendent or the Other—has been converted into the historical category of hope and is treated as "An Image of the Future" in the Conclusion to our work.

If we have devoted more space to our analysis of *Seven Beauties* than to any other Wertmüller film, it is our formal way of expressing meaning: Length should indicate our estimate of its proportionate greatness in her works to date. Although at this writing it is the full flower of her earlier films, our hope can only be that it is actually one of many that have yet to bloom.

Part One
The Artist and Her World

Mimi (Giancarlo Giannini) and friend (Luigi Diberti) in *The Seduction of Mimi*.

"I have always been struck by the parable of the talents in the Gospel, of the wonderful opportunity given exclusively to man to invest as best he can the coin of life. As a consequence, I am also struck by every neglect and every waste."[1] With sentiments such as these Lina Wertmüller explains, in part, the fecundity of her art over the past decade and a half and the social concern that permeates it.

Arcangela Wertmüller von Elgg was born in Rome in 1932 of a family that had its origins in Zurich, Switzerland.[2] "My great-great-grandfather was no less than the Baron Erich Wertmüller von Elgg, but I am a Roman of Rome."[3] The early years of her education were spent in a convent school, where at thirteen years of age she questioned the religious context in which it was received. She had no use for an omniscient God who could give human beings free will and then create a hell for them to fall into. "On this point I fought with everybody, with all the priests and all the nuns, and I broke my link with the Church."[4]

Her interest in writing and directing began to develop very soon after the Second World War. Except for one course in directing, she had no formal training but learned her art mainly by doing. For a time she traveled all over Italy with Maria Signorelli's puppet troupe. "Hand puppets," she says, preferring them to marionettes because they are more human and, in the use of the hands, more Italian.[5] But the puppet shows were not always viewed with favor: Mothers brought their children to see Punch and Judy and they got Kafka. In 1951 she founded, with some friends, an avant-garde theater, though now she thinks of the adventure as "rearguard." Its chances for success were never very great, mainly because the early fifties were a time when the Italian film industry was burgeoning and the new Cinecittà proved to be irresistible for the members of her company—and eventually for her too.

For a number of years she was much more engaged in writing

for the media than directing for it. In 1954 she had the good fortune of collaborating with the top-notch writing team of Garinei and Giovannini, who wrote musical comedies for Italian television. Over the years she worked with them on more than a dozen shows while continuing to work for radio and in theater. She wrote two plays for the stage; one of them, *Two and Two Are No Longer Four* (1968), became a hit, and little wonder. Franco Zeffirelli directed it, Enrico Job did the sets and costumes, and Giancarlo Giannini starred in it. Wertmüller and Job have since married; he is the superbly competent art director of her films now. And when Wertmüller was ready to start on *The Seduction of Mimi* (1971), Giannini too was happily seduced into a collaboration that has endured to this day.

Their friendship had begun almost a decade earlier in 1963, when Wertmüller saw Giannini play Puck in *A Midsummer Night's Dream*. Even though he was only twenty, Giannini was already recognized as one of the finest young stage actors in Italy. He worked with Wertmüller for the first time in 1966 when she directed a film called *Rita the Mosquito* under the pseudonym "George Brown." "More than anybody," Enrico Job admits, "it was Giancarlo who helped Lina to launch into films, introducing her to producers, backers and so on. Without him, she would probably still be waiting for a chance."[6]

It was Flora Mastroianni, however, Marcello's wife and a friend of Wertmüller's from her convent school days, who introduced her to Fellini. Fellini made her his assistant on *8½* (1962), but as soon as she got backing to do a film of her own she parted from him amicably and even persuaded him to release some of his crew on *8½* to go with her to Sicily for the filming. The working title of this first film was *Oblomov di provinica* but she changed it to *I Basilischi (The Lizards)* to indicate, she says, "the reactionary apathy of some zones of southern Italy in analogy with the typical immobility of lizards in the sun."[7] Released in 1963, it was a critical and popular success and established her as one of the few women to achieve recognition as a film director. She is, moreover, one of the few directors who is also her own scriptwriter. This fact accounts for the development of theme in the body of her work; it is one good reason for the writing of this book.

Her cinema is notable for its political character. In every film, she says, she tries to make her audiences aware that *they* are society, that they are all responsible, that they must use their heads or perish. "It is indispensable to distinguish between true and false development, between progress and illusion, between word and message."[8] Her protagonist is the common man, a citizen of that third world that every society, even the most developed, nourishes in its midst. "My man of the South . . . in his dealings with politics, industrial society, and sex, isn't tied to a specific provincial region. This is what the Americans have understood."[9] It is a mistake, she believes, to imagine oneself to be the victim of a hostile society and for that reason to give up trying to change things. The extent of that mistake in imagination is portrayed with power in *The Seduction of Mimi*.

Politically, Wertmüller is a socialist, but an Italian socialist, and more precisely still, a Mancini socialist. Lucy Quacinella, an assistant to Wertmüller on *Swept Away*, expresses it this way: "In the extraordinary realm of Italian politics, her official political stance is not very far to the left of center. Giacomo Mancini, leader of the conservative faction of a by no means revolutionary Socialist Party, is Lina's political idol. The Italian Socialists favor a program even more reform-oriented than the Communists." Wertmüller's socialism is not identified with the "proletarian masses"; it is a socialism that remains deeply concerned with individual freedom. "I believe in the individual," she herself says, "and it is the Italian Socialist Party (in contrast to the Communists and the Social Democrats, who are concerned only with industrial mass society) that is concerned with the freedom of the individual." Her films could not be clearer or more consistent in portraying and deploring the systems that stifle that freedom. Yet in the final analysis the political tone of her films seems closer somehow to Chaplin than it does to Costa-Gavras. "Ideology," she told John Simon, "must not devour, but illuminate, art."[10]

It is clear that the discussion of theme in her movies, including their political implications, places them at a level rivaling the best in recent cinema. Great art, of course, transcends the particular; it reaches the heart of everyone. Critics have found this universal appeal in Wertmüller's films. Although at this point, there is scarcely any consensus about their meaning, there is a regrettable tendency to interpret them pessimistically. Lillian Gerard, for example, finds a recurring theme to be "the absurdity of a man's predicament": "While he pretends outwardly to be in command of his destiny, he experiences within a fear and trembling that come from his anxiety over being alone, his fear of being abandoned, his expectation of bodily harm, and his knowledge of impending death. All are fears that he cannot reconcile and so he denies them, and instead cherishes false virtues, dignity, pride, self-importance, and an inflated idea of his own potency." Penelope Gilliatt expresses theme in Wertmüller simply in terms of a recurring question, "How are we to live together?" Diane Jacobs feels that Wertmüller explores a variety of pragmatic answers to that question: "survival through living," "capitulation," "molding oneself to society." Brooks Riley finds "messages" lurking behind almost every change of scene in her films, but then mentions only one explicitly: The "grim" and "cynical" message of *Seven Beauties,* he claims, is "survival first."[11]

Wertmüller's reception by American audiences, all since 1974, has been something of a phenomenon. And although not all, by any means, have fallen in line, American critics too have been lavish in their praise. Commenting in more ways than one on the quality of that reception, a Roman journalist has referred to Wertmüller as "Santa Lina di New York." The Italian press, it would seem, is still baffled by the extent of her acclaim here and slow to give her the praise she deserves. Quacinella attempts an answer to both sides, yet reveals her Roman bias: "Americans have considered Italy's critical rejection of Wertmüller's work either as an enormous oversight, a bizarre case of cultural myopia, or as the result of some national inability to accept a negative image of themselves. But it's more likely the case that America is suffering from a lack in political perspective that makes it easy to be taken in—from the Left as well as dead center—by the brilliance of a highly polished and well packaged product."[12] Quacinella is apparently unfamiliar with the political impact of recent American films like Ashby's *Shampoo* (1975), Altman's *Nashville* (1975), and Pakula's *All the President's Men* (1976). Moreover, Wertmüller's are not the first foreign films with a political slant left of center to be well received here. *Film Comment* ran opposing views of Wertmüller in a 1976 issue. While Diane Jacobs suggests she may be an "Italian Aristophanes," Brooks Riley insists that she is "a clever, energetic, daring, and competent boulevard director—an Italianate Normal Lear with some of the censorship taken out." Commenting on her visual aesthetic, Riley calls her "expedient and sloppy" and "an overeager synthesizer, [who's] gotten something from everyone: characters and comic grotesques from Fellini, theatrical lighting from Visconti, satire from de Filippo, that concentration-camp blue from Cavani." (A more constructive statement can and will be made about her indebtedness to other Italian film artists.) Michael Wood finds that her "style alternates like her moods, by sudden switches from long shot to close-up, with nothing in between." Then, damning with faint praise, he concedes that "the good moments in Wertmüller's movies are always moments of abrupt, stylish flamboyance." Pauline Kael, deploring the "absence of weight" in the climactic sequences of *Seven Beauties,* labels her "a playwright-director" whose "scripts are a succession of dialogue scenes in which characters give bent to ideological positions." Tom Allen, on the other hand, finds her "a beguilingly instinctual entertainer-director" who "has willfully chosen to come on strong like a psychic vaudevillian with a cosmic rubber bladder."[13]

There has been no praise among American critics, however, to rival John Simon's. "If *Swept Away* marks a considerable step beyond Wertmüller's earlier, very fine films, *Seven Beauties,*" he proclaims, "is an upward leap in seven-league boots that propels her into the highest regions of cinematic art, into the company of the major directors." Simon discerns three kinds of great artists: the exquisitely tasteful within limitations, artists who transcend known boundaries, and "a rare third kind that combines aspects of the two divergent greatnesses—artists who are, somehow, both big and small, fierce and civilized, beyond taste and yet also, miraculously, tasteful." For Simon, *Seven Beauties,* is "the work of this third kind of artist."[14] Although his language is surely excessive and his judgment a bit premature, his enthusiasm is understandable and his critical sensibilities basically sound.

True art does not of course appear full blown. It develops, as its creator does, on its own native soil, the heir of an artistic tradition. If Wertmüller is lately approaching the international stature of some of her fellow directors—Fellini, Visconti, Pasolini, de Sica, Bertolucci—it is not without at least a general indebtedness to the cinematic heritage they have created. The love of her country—the shape of the land, the look of its people, and the endurance of its art—is as evident in her films as it is in Fellini's. She shares many of the thematic concerns of her country's great directors. "This brilliant, very original Italian director," Vincent Canby writes, ". . . has taken the social-sexual-political concerns of a lot of other filmmakers—including Fellini, Visconti, and de Sica—and turned them into visions—both comic and poetic—unlike the work of anyone else." Even those who are critical of her vision compare her with Italy's best. "Wertmüller, like Bertolucci," Michael Wood says, "has a stunning visual intelligence accompanied by a great confusion of mind." Molly Haskell, who regards her as a male chauvinist of the most insidious kind, nevertheless considers her films "an attempt to fuse Pasolini's proletarian parables with Fellini's lyricism."[15]

Her mastery of the medium seems beyond question. Like all true film artists, she depends on the strength of the image rather than the power of words. John Simon comments on her technical expertise: "Wertmüller is a master both of camera placement and movement, and of editing, or montage. She would have delighted Bazin as much as Eisenstein." Later in the same essay, he exclaims simply: "What sense of detail!"[16] Other critics note her poetic use of colors, her sense of the power of silence, the agility of her visual style. Enrico Job, her husband and art director, clearly shares these honors with her.

Wertmüller describes the artistic process as a "long love." *Love* applied to art is surely a metaphor; its need to persevere through the rigors of creation, a reality. "To make a movie, to do anything big in life, you have to start with a very special love or

The Artist and Her World

a very special anger and be able to keep it going and finish with the same feeling." It is just such an anger that persists even through the frenzied comic style of *All Screwed Up,* exploding at the end just short of revolution. Or one can start with a feeling for the kind of "light and love inside a man" that makes him undertake an impossible, even senseless task.[17] This sort of feeling, she declares, prompted the "long love" that became *Love and Anarchy.*

Her aim is forever to incite and provoke. It is this dimension of her art that is the substance of parable. The very furor she has created in the press supports the parabolic interpretation of her films. Even the annoyance that some of her severest critics have expressed, in this country as well as in her own, is evidence of the fact that they have been disturbed—at some level of perception or psyche—by her art. If her art is indeed the art of parable, then we can expect resistance. Parable is the mode of prophets.[18]

Part Two
The Parables of Lina Wertmüller

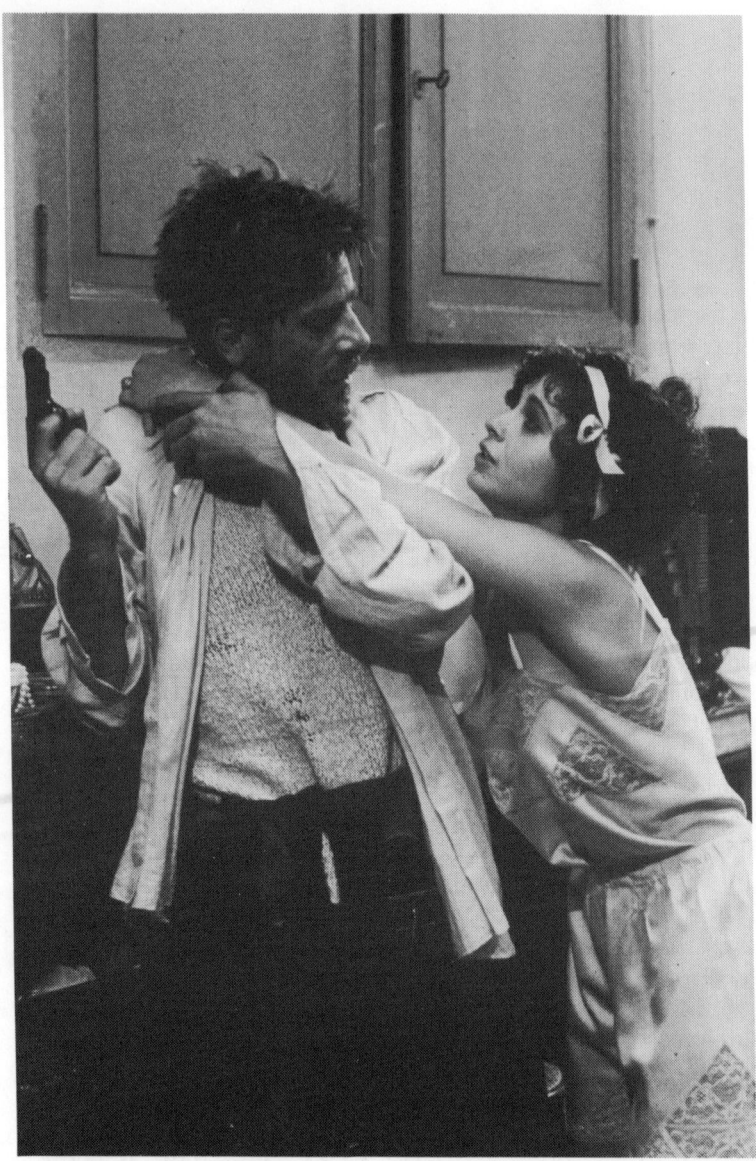

Tunin (Giancarlo Giannini) and Tripolina (Lina Polito) in *Love and Anarchy*.

I
Images of World

Suppose the story of Genesis had been set in a cave instead of in a garden. Would it have made any difference? Of course it would have. If the story is going to deal effectively with a world lost and a world (to be) regained, it must be given a setting that suggests a world worth having. The garden is an image of world that implies both cultivation and bounty. Shakespeare uses it later on in *Richard II* to show what Richard's kingdom is not. Of course, the *kind* of garden can make a difference too: Behind the Italians' peculiar passion for the geometrically patterned garden, Barzini detects fear—fear of the uncontrollable in nature.[1] An image of world is essential to any dramatic work. The more precise the better. Because film deals so radically with a profusion of images, precision is all the more necessary. On the stage, select images must be carefully planted; on the screen, images must be weeded out so that the select will appear. Images of world emerge as the camera focuses with increasing regularity on this or that aspect of physical reality. In all her films Lina Wertmüller is clear about what images of world she requires to give her stories their proper setting.

The main image of world in *The Seduction of Mimi* is quite the opposite of a garden: It is a quarry, and it figures importantly at the beginning, the middle, and the end of the film. At the beginning of the film, Mimi (short for Carmelo) is seen among the laborers there, who are being told from a Mafia sound-car which candidate to vote for. Politically, they are at the mercy of the Mafia; Mimi knows it, and the quarry might just as well be his prison. The aridity of it follows him even into his home: Sexually, he is at the mercy of his frigid wife, and like the Mafia she has none. Forced out of his job for voting Communist, he leaves for Turin where he trains for a job as a skilled metalworker and falls in love with a girl named Fiore. They have a child, but soon after the Mafia maneuvers him back to Catania, and there his exaggerated sense of honor puts him in such a quandary he ends up in the quarry again. It is in the quarry that he learns that his wife's frigidity has melted long enough for her to get pregnant by another man—a customs officer who is already married and has five children. To restore his wounded honor in the eyes of the world—the Sicilian world, that is— Mimi seduces Amalia, the officer's ungainly wife, and gets *her* pregnant. But the Mafia steps in and does him the "favor" of killing off the sergeant; Mimi, of course, goes to jail. When he gets out, thanks again to the Mafia, he is greeted by the cries of seven children—the sergeant's five, his one by Amalia, and the one that Fiore's love had given him. Now he must support them all. The Mafia has him where they want him—in the quarry, this time *in* the sound-car, from which *he* now harangues the workers. This is the seduction of Mimi. The last image we see is of the quarry: Fiore, bitterly disappointed in Mimi, driving off with a friend in a van festooned with Maoist banners and Mimi like a bug in a vast desert calling after her, desperately trying to justify himself. The quarry becomes an image of Mimi's world—an arid world without love, a world scooped out for the building of worlds not his, a world of isolation to which his own folly has condemned him.

Isolation in *Swept Away* is of another kind. Set adrift in a dinghy, a man and a woman find themselves literally marooned on an island. Raffaella is an upper-class bitch, Gennarino is a working-class bastard. The island has nothing to offer unless you know how to get at it. Gennarino knows how; Rafaella is helpless. The absolute male, which had always struggled to emerge in Gennarino but which circumstances had in one way or another forced him to suppress, now declares itself in all its reactionary power. The island becomes an image of his fantasy world. Raffaella had treated him like dirt when he had to serve her on the pleasure yacht from which they had strayed; now he would set things right. Not only would she be made to serve his every need, she must be brought to *want* to serve him, to hunger for his domination over her. She must, in fact, begin to see in him her god. It is granted only to a few to happen upon an island where fantasies can be cultivated undisturbed. But how do you test the reality of a fantasy? You bring it into the real world, of course. That is just what Gennarino does, and alas, it was only a fantasy after all!

But what if the real world becomes itself a fantasy world? The Italy of Mussolini was such a fantasy world, an excrescence of the absolute male in him. In *Love and Anarchy* Lina Wertmüller plants another fantasy world within that world: a brothel. Genet in *The Balcony* uses the brothel to mirror the world outside where the acts of men are doomed to eternal repetition; Wertmüller uses it not only to mirror the world of Mussolini's Italy, but ironically to provide a place for a new political reality to be born. Anarchy is supposed to preside over its birth, but love subverts it. Perhaps the implication is that until love becomes political and politics loving there can be no new reality. When Tunin, a simple peasant, comes to the brothel in Rome, he asks for Salome, one of the whores. She is to be his contact, his companion in anarchy; with her help he will assassinate Mussolini. But he meets Tripolina, and she becomes his companion in love. To keep him for herself, Tripolina opposes Salome. When Salome capitulates and allows Tunin to sleep beyond the appointed hour, the attempt to dissolve the fantasy world outside is itself dissolved in the fantasy world of the brothel.

A totalitarian world creates concentration camps in order to banish all undesirable elements from the paradise it imagines it is building on earth; in so doing, it creates perfect images of the hell it actually is. The concentration camp carries the fantasies of the absolute male to their absurd conclusion. There is no virtue in absolute maleness, just as there is no virtue in absolute femaleness. *In media stat virtus*, in the assimilation of the feminine into masculinity and the assimilation of the masculine into femininity. What an irony to find that in the concentration camp of *Seven Beauties* the supreme devil is a woman! She is what we shall later call a ballbuster; when a ballbuster is at the height of her power she is a parody of the absolute male, and when a man's balls are broken by such a woman he is reduced to a parody of the absolute female. This is exactly what happens to Pasqualino when he comes up against the commandant in *Seven Beauties*. In his passion to survive, by ruses born of desperation, he prostitutes himself to her. So much for the superiority of the penis. With the human species there is no Darwinian law that says only the superior must survive. What constitutes superiority in the human species? Concentration camps are founded on the premise that somebody knows. The commandant thought she knew. All devils are finally deceived.

If *Seven Beauties* is Wertmüller's *Inferno*, *All Screwed Up* is her *Ante-Purgatorio,* imaged in the kitchen of a Milanese restaurant. In its own way her film, in the end, begins to describe the action that preoccupies Dante throughout his poem: a search for the better. In *Seven Beauties* Wertmüller extracts comedy out of a tragic situation; in *All Screwed Up* she implies tragedy in a comic situation.[2] All the characters in *All Screwed Up* are more or less in the same situation. Most of them are country people come to the city. All of them are trying to better their situations. That is why they came to the city in the first place. They form a kind of commune in an old tenement building quaintly out of place in the middle of modern Milan, a precarious perch in a city on fire with its own unregulated progress. All of them fall into the fire, victims of a modern Moloch, of the consumer society that demands their absolute obeisance.

There is Isotta (Isa Danieli), who resorts to prostitution in order to support herself and all her relatives back home; there is Sante (Claudio Volontè) and his dream bride Marluccia (Lina Polito), whose marital union erupts beyond control with a sudden rash of children, first twins, then quintuplets, and God knows what next; there is Adelina (Sara Rapisarda), a frightened pip of a girl who becomes as fearless as an acrobat in her scramble up the economic ladder, never mind whose fingers she mashes on the way (even loving fingers); there is Gigi (Luigi Diberti), who falls in with the Salvador Dali of the underworld, making quick money by enacting symbolic vengeances (like painting a police car with shit) and learning to rob with finesse. There is actually no one central character in this film. As in Eisenstein's *Strike,* its principal character is the whole mass of workers, southern Italians come to the industrial North. But if any character can be said to be allotted more than equal time, it would be Carletto (Nino Bignamini). He arrives from the country with Gigi and meets Adelina when she is still that frightened pip of a girl in the train station. He falls in love with her and wants to marry her, but by this time she is already on her way up the money tree, and she will not hear of marriage until Carletto makes enough to satisfy her rising level of consumption. Carletto goes from job to job. His first is in a meat-packing plant where the camera introduces us to the great consumer society by orchestrating the slaughter of bulls to the measured time of a baroque concerto, a counterpoint of flesh and spirit. Punctuating the rhythm are shots of the eyes of bulls, fixed in death, an allusion perhaps to the last shot in Eisenstein's *Strike:* the eye of a slaughtered bull, followed by a quotation about workers still suffering all over the world.[3] But the plant is soon involved in a labor dispute, and Carletto is out on the street again. Unblemished victim that he is, he ends up—yes, in that kitchen of a Milanese restaurant.

We never see the restaurant, but if the kitchen is any indication, it must be the biggest and the busiest in the world. The kitchen is, of course, the world of this film. The ovens blaze away like hellmouths. The workers in this kitchen, men and women, act as if they are under orders to feed the Imperial Army on the eve of combat. Indeed their chief has something of a martinet about him. Or of the impresario pulling out his hair over a company of prima donnas who stamp their feet and refuse to come to order. A pretense of order masks the unrest momentarily when the owner of the restaurant, an old lady dressed in black, is wheeled through the kitchen by her son. Then a bomb explodes in the restaurant—no doubt a fascist provocation—and a riot quickly erupts in the street. Justice is caught napping again, of course: Sante is arrested by mistake. The waiters seize the opportunity to avenge their plight; they dunk the owner's son's head in a pot of sauce. Carletto is caught somewhere in the middle of it all. "Maybe we should stop," he cries, "and start again in a different place!" And suddenly everything does stop—except the camera, which patrols the aisles of the kitchen past faces frozen in contemplation of a future yet unseen. Then someone reminds the workers that people are outside, waiting to be served, and the vicious cycle of motion begins all over again. The camera pans the room, slowly, completely; it sweeps everything up into its spin as it pans again and again, faster each time, until the screen is streaked by a dizzying swirl of images and the film ends abruptly with everything literally "all screwed up," or as the Italian title has it: "everything in place but nothing in working order."

The quarry, the island, the brothel, the concentration camp, the restaurant kitchen—these are the settings that Wertmüller has chosen for some of her best scripts. The setting of a film is not unlike what St. Ignatius Loyola in his *Spiritual Exercises* calls a composition of place. It gathers the mind and readies the heart for action. In the meditation on sin, for instance, the exercitant is asked to imagine his soul in the cage of his body and his entire being in exile, as it were, among wild beasts. This is not the whole of reality; in fact, it is an image of world as seen through a distorted lens. But that is why it serves for the meditation on sin: Both psychologically and theologically, it begins to say what sin does. Wertmüller's images of world are like that; they do not show us the whole of reality, but they begin to tell us what happens when our instinct for absolutizing comes into conflict with our instinct for survival, sometimes within the soul, sometimes between souls.

Wertmüller's images of world do not necessarily generate despair. But neither do they celebrate hope. In all of her films if we look beyond the particular image there is the city, which is sometimes mirrored by that image or which sometimes becomes itself a mirror of a different aspect of world. In *The Seduction of Mimi* Catania is a city where "no one minds his own business." In *Swept Away* all the talk aboard the pleasure yacht is city talk, and the Italian ship of state is like nothing so much as a ship of fools.[4] Rome in *Love and Anarchy* is a monument to Mussolini; in *Seven Beauties* Naples is turned into a brothel. Finally, in *All Screwed Up,* Milan is all stomach; it consumes everything. Where is the city of the future, the Arcosanti, the dream city such as the one that Paolo Soleri is building in the Arizona desert? Not all dreams deserve to become reality. Like most of us, Wertmüller is waiting to dream the right dream. The prophet's dream in the Book of Revelation is of the New Jerusalem, radiant as a bride, where all people shall live in harmony with themselves, with others, and with God.

II
Images of Woman

Most feminists will have none of her. Ellen Willis claims that she "is not only a female woman hater—a type that has actually surpassed the Jewish anti-Semite in popularity—but a woman hater who pretends to be a feminist." She is not your average woman hater, Willis maintains; "she has what amounts to an obsessional conviction that women have no souls." According to Molly Haskell, she is the most experienced woman filmmaker working today, but she is also "the one who least identifies with the concerns and interests of the women's movement, from which she has repeatedly dissociated herself, proclaiming the 'androgyny' of the artist."[1]

What does Lina Wertmüller say about herself? She insists she has genuine feminist sentiments. She has told John Simon that on seventy or eighty percent of their demands she is with the feminists "to the death," but the important thing is to be a human being. In an interview with Paul McIsaac and Gina Blumenfeld, she points to her feminist film *Let's Talk About Men* and says of the characters in *Love and Anarchy:* "These are very strong women; they instinctively rebel against militarism and the patriarchal order. Why are these women never mentioned by the feminist critics?" Finally, she suggests that these same critics take a good look at the *men* in her films. "Think how they are portrayed," she is reported saying. "All vain, arrogant and stupid, real chauvinists who believe in the superiority of the penis."[2]

What images of women are we given? Some critics may prefer to say, what types? *Type is* not that bad a word. The men and women of the commedia dell'arte are stock characters, types; later dramatists, beginning with Goldoni, took these same characters and made them persons. Wertmüller comes out of a theatrical tradition that is unmistakably Italian. Stock characters abound in her films, but if they are in any way central to the story they begin to emerge, *in situation,* as persons.

One image that presents itself is woman as *victim.* There is a sense in which all the characters in *All Screwed Up,* both men and women, are victims, victims of the consumer society that catches them up, just as the camera does at the end, in a vortex of its own making. But the biggest victims turn out to be Sante and his wife Marluccia. She, above all. When we first meet her, Marluccia is a lovely young girl with long blond hair and a bright smile. She is looking over her shoulder at a young mustachioed man who has been watching her with adoring eyes as she dresses a mannequin in a department store window. They begin to date, and all too soon she is with child. Only it turns out to be twins. Wife and mother, she must quit her job to mind the children, while he, a poor Sicilian just come to Milan, must find what work he can. She is on the pill now, but either it backfires or she forgets to take it because she becomes pregnant again and this time gives birth to quintuplets! In the antepilulian era,[3] with the right kind of publicity, that might have meant money, but multiple birth is too common now for the media to take notice. By this time her hair is cropped and lightless, her eyes sunken and red from crying.

To feed his brood, Sante works day and night, so tired that he can hardly keep his eyes open. We come upon him at his job one night trying to paint a dividing line down the middle of the road; it looks rather like a white snake inching its way to the other side. In desperation he even tries male prostitution. Coat and tie, red flower in buttonhole, he waits for a likely customer. An apparently high living woman pulls up in a car. He gets in beside her. "Twenty thousand lire," he says, "payable in advance." The woman agrees to the contract, and both at the same time hold out their hands to receive the money. Michael Wood comments: "It's hard to think of a funnier, more intelligent image of what it means to compete for the same economic space."[4] He might have added: even to the point of equalizing the sexes.

But Marluccia, mother of seven, has not seen the end of it. While both are victimized by the economy, she is also victimized by his male desire. In one scene in which he falls exhausted into bed beside her, he turns to her for sex. She begs him not to. He becomes angry: "You can't refuse me this!" Somebody is lacking in imagination. The upshot of it all is she gets pregnant again. Without telling him, she allows herself to be taken to an underground abortion clinic. As a kind of front or merely as ironic commentary, a Renaissance madonna and child is hanging on the wall. The mother-to-be (or not-to-be) looks up at the painting with guilt and fear in her eyes. When another woman emerges from her ordeal physically and emotionally ill, hustled away even though she requires medical attention, the already burdened Marluccia decides she will go ahead and bear her eighth child (supposing, of course, that she carries no more than one child in her womb), bemoaning the fact that this kind of clinic should have to exist, "all because the government disapproves."[5]

Two other women in *All Screwed Up* can be considered victims: Isotta, who resorts to prostitution (she says) to support her mother and brother and sisters, and Adelina, who arrived from Sicily all atremble but has since found a perch on the economic ladder comfortable enough to support a TV set. When Carletto, the young man she loves but will not marry and will not sleep with until they do marry, determines to have her anyway, she struggles against him in a locked room, knocks over her TV set, catches it as it teeters at the edge of the table, but is unable from her prone position to set it right again. Should she let it drop and protect her virginity or . . .? The grin on Carletto's face says all.

Victim, indeed, but the image of woman that Adelina best represents is that of the *tease*. Carletto is a decent sort. He wants desperately to marry the girl, but she will not hear of it, for the simple reason that he is not making enough money to maintain the standard of living that she has come to expect. "Look at Sante and his wife," she says, as if every woman gives multiple birth at the drop of her panty hose (which Adelina has taken to wearing), with or without the pill. Still, Carletto remains faithful; he is not like his friend Gigi, who takes advantage of every woman he can lay his hands on. Ironically, it is Sante, that desperate father of seven, so shy and so full of *cortesía*, who "inspires" the rape that puts an end to Adelina's teasing.

Related (in Carletto's eyes) to woman as tease are those inaccessible women whom he glimpses from a distance at intervals throughout the film. It is the economic spectrum that makes them inaccessible. They stand at the other end, and to the sound of music they glance at him as if from the ad of some rare perfume, beckoning and forbidding at the same time.

Lina Wertmüller looks beyond the sober succession of doctors and lawyers through which she is descended to the great-great-grandfather who fled Switzerland after fighting a duel over a woman and announces proudly: "I'm the last ballbuster left."[6] One is not surprised, therefore, to meet in her films the image of woman as *ballbuster*. What is surprising is to find these ballbusters so different from her and from one another. The only common denominator seems to be that they will stand up to any man and, if need be, make him wilt beneath their gaze. The three ballbusters that converge on this one point before they go their very separate ways are the commandant in *Seven Beauties,* Amalia in *The Seduction of Mimi,* and Raffaella in *Swept Away.*

"They've broken my balls," the anarchist in *Seven Beauties* says. Now it appears to be Pasqualino's turn. The camera looks down at him from a high angle over the back and shoulder of the seated commandant. To Pasqualino, the commandant is a huge and forbidding mountain. Dare he attempt to climb her? That would be "heroism of a sort," Michael Wood declares, "but we have only to substitute a beautiful and slender camp commandant for the large Shirley Stoler to see how offensively trivial a notion of heroism it is—not comic, merely sniggering."[7] If we are going to speak of heroism at all, the substitution would render his "heroism" perhaps less comic but no less remarkable. It is not the *size* of the ballbuster that intimidates so much as her *contempt.* Whether justified or not, contempt is her principal weapon. When the commandant orders Pasqualino to drop his pants and with a cold deliberation parts his shirt to inspect his penis, it is the gaze that withers, the gaze of a woman who, shapely or not, has over him the power of life and death. But even a ballbuster can have something of the victim about her. Pasqualino hardly knows what he says when he blurts out: "Maybe you're a victim of your sense of duty."

One may ask if Amalia, the ballbuster in *The Seduction of Mimi,* is not also a victim of her sense of duty. It is clear that she has only contempt for her husband, whom she was forced to marry when he got her pregnant. She is busily raising her five children when Mimi comes upon the scene, intent upon her seduction as a way of getting back at her husband for having had the temerity to seduce his wife Rosalia in the cabin of a crane. At first Amalia shows him the contempt he deserves, but then, falling victim to the simple hope that she may indeed be attractive to a man, she lets herself be courted. When he attempts to rape her, she puts up an incredible fight, giving in only when he assures her that he cannot live without her.

Where the commandant was a passive mountain daring Pasqualino to scale her, Amalia is a great wall ready to fall upon the man who dares huddle in her shadow. Contempt, through deception, has been temporarily submerged in this ballbuster (it will surface later with a vengeance); he may not wilt before her gaze but he does indeed wilt before her size. The camera has us confront through Mimi's eyes what is about to befall him; but then, mercilessly, it turns its own fish eyes upon Amalia from the rear. Wertmüller elephantisizes Amalia's swaying butt, in all the glory of its nakedness, to such a degree that one can only gasp and exclaim in dismay—not so much at the actress' butt as at the director's effrontery. But then we hear the director say of herself: "It's not so terrible to be ridiculous—I am living proof of this point. I've always been a character, a clown. I'm like the big ass in *Mimi.*"[8]

But Amalia the ballbuster has her day. No doubt ballbusters get most of their power through men's stupid vanity. When Mimi emerges from prison, Amalia descends upon him with all her children (there are six now), and in order to support them, he is forced to capitulate to the Mafia, that most practiced ballbuster of them all.

The woman who enrages the feminists more than any other of Wertmüller's creations is Raffaella in *Swept Away.* When we

Images of Woman

first meet her monarchizing like a Cleopatra on her barge, she is aptly described as "the biggest ballbuster at sea." But when, like Cleopatra, she becomes a slave to passion and makes a mere man her king, in the eyes of the feminists she can only be regarded as a traitor to the realm. No, not she, but Wertmüller, who makes her do the things she does. Wertmüller, however, also brings her through the last episode of the film, a right reading of which discloses a Raffaella rather different from the ballbuster of the beginning and the blissful slave of the middle.

The atmosphere on the pleasure yacht in the Mediterranean is charged from the very start, setting up a magnetic field between the man and the woman. Even as they repulse one another, the forces of a strange attraction are building. What is Gennarino (Giancarlo Giannini) but a cabin boy, a sailor of sorts who makes his living by serving Raffaella (Mariangela Melato) and her rich and powerful friends? A Communist himself, he seethes as he overhears her pontificating about the superiority of capitalism over socialism, complaining all the while about the warmed-over coffee and the overcooked spaghetti and the over-ripe smell of his shirt. It is he who at a late hour is ordered to take her in a dinghy to join some of her friends who had left earlier for a swim at a grotto. As they start out, the magnetic field begins to crackle. However, when the motor conks out and they are faced with the prospect of drifting all night, she is not in the least apprehensive that he will take advantage of the situation. Queen that she is, she falls asleep under his gaze, but not before tossing him a few more insults, every one of which he catches and carefully stores away in his turbulent brain, as if half-suspecting that the very forces of repulsion that drive them apart will one day bring them clashingly together.

That day comes all too soon, when having lost their way they beach upon an island. At first, Raffaella imagines that nothing has changed: She is still the master, he is still the slave. She *must* have some coffee—"iced, of course." When his explorations make it all too clear that the island is deserted, he calls back to her from a high rock: "About that coffee—I'm afraid it's going to be a problem!" The verbal exchanges between the two, while they are often funny, are always tense, rising as they do out of an interplay between sexism and class prejudice, between sexual and political power. So long as they were on the yacht (that extension of the capitalist world), politics was the power base even for sex: She could dominate him as the "biggest ballbuster at sea." But now on the island, where there are no capitalist structures to provide for their needs, male assumes dominance over female, and his sexual power becomes all the political power he needs. The irony here is that ordinarily it is precisely *within* capitalist structures that male assumes dominance over female, both sexually and politically; but apparently to call attention to the situation, Wertmüller inverts it: "In this film, the woman represents the bourgeoisie and the man represents the third world, those who are indeed helpless. In actuality, she represents men and he represents women."[9] But Wertmüller does not accurately assess her achievement when, in the same interview, she says of her intentions that *Swept Away* is "not a comment on the relation of the sexes but on the power relations between social classes." It cannot help but be a comment on the relation of the sexes, for it is *through* that relationship that the director is able to make her statement about the relationship of social classes.

Gennarino sets about the task of living. Raffaella curses. "There must be a restaurant, a motel, at least a cafe!" But the camera circling from above belies her hopes. He catches a lobster, cooks and eats it, then throws what is left on the fire. Desperate with hunger, she berates him for his selfishness. He answers: "I'm just doing what you rich people do when you burn food to keep the prices up." If she wants to eat, she is going to have to work for her dinner. Gennarino is not about to wait on her. In fact, she must wait on him, and she can start by washing his pants. Hunger forces her to capitulate, and even though she hates doing it she washes his pants. He kicks her for her trouble, determined to break her spirit. Now he flings back at her all those insults he had fielded, punctuating them with physical blows, building up to that shocking scene where he sends her reeling under his attack, pursuing her and finally subduing her. As he is about to rape her, he demands that she admit it is just what she wants, that she admit the passion she feels for him now. But suddenly he releases her, saying: "No! Passion is not enough. You have to love me. I've got to become your god!" One's feelings at this point are ambivalent, to say the least. Wertmüller has said that though sadomasochism may be a very important element in eroticism, her movies are never erotic.[10] She is (partly) wrong about sadomasochism, unless we are willing to say that the only valid meaning of eroticism implies the abnormal; she is (mostly) right about her films, because there is usually too much else going on.[11] Nevertheless, the scene in *Swept Away* just described is sexually exciting; it thereby creates a conflict in the viewer. While instinct inclines toward consummation, the mind revolts against exploitation. Later on, when Raffaella identifies with a rabbit that Gennarino skins and skewers, one is reminded of a scene in Ugo Betti's *The Fugitive*. The husband, thinking of his guilty wife fleeing before an inexorable justice, tells of having once seen a trembling rabbit caught in a hunter's trap: "I was for the rabbit," he says.

At that stage when the ballbuster is herself completely busted, she declares her love for the man who has enslaved her. She kisses his feet, surrenders her body to him, garlands his loins with flowers. This is not just another taming of the shrew, as some critics have suggested; Petruchio was never Kate's unwilling servant. Nor is it an exact reversal of the master-slave relationship: When Raffaella held the whip over Gennarino, there was no love between them even if there was a perverse attraction; now that Gennarino holds the whip, there *is* love—not only her love for him but his love for her. Enslaving her he becomes her slave. They are both swept away by an unusual passion in the blue sea of August, as we see very graphically in the shot that has become the film's publicity still, showing Gennarino and Rafaella locked in one another's arms with the sea breaking over them. "We end up adoring the very thing we struggled against," says Teilhard de Chardin.[12] On the sexual level, she is woman adoring her first "real man," but it is class politics that makes her think this way. High society makes mice of men. On the political level, he is the proletariat adoring bourgeois values, but it is sexual politics that makes him think that way. The "inaccessible" becomes graspable in her.

It is absurd to think that Wertmüller is saying that what happens on the island is the natural state of things, that on this "small paradise" of an island we have an image of what Adam and Eve were meant to be before society corrupted them. Society is itself an expression of nature. As William Golding suggests in the island setting of his *Lord of the Flies,* society comes to be with the good and the bad, and the good and the bad are rooted in human nature. He suggests further, in keeping with the Judaeo-Christian tradition, that ours is a fallen nature. Fallen nature, phenomenologically speaking, is an evolving nature, and society is the instrument of that evolution. It is clear that the state of things on the island comes about *in reaction to* the state of things as they existed on the boat. One form of society gives way to another, and because they are both extremes neither is the ideal instrument. What we sense at the end of the film is precisely an awareness of this fact.

The end is precipitated by the sighting of the boat that marks the dividing line between the two forms of society. As Carolyn Porter and Paul Thomas describe the scene, "Wertmüller orchestrates distance, desire, threat and recognition in a series of quick cuts as Rafaella and Gennarino look at each other from afar to decide whether the ship should be signalled."[13] Over her objections, he opts for rescue. He convinces himself that it is not enough for Raffaella to declare her love for him in the narrow world that brought them together; she must declare it in the larger world that kept them apart. Machismo needs not so much the eyes of the woman tyrannized as the eyes of other men.

But Raffaella *knows.* She knows that once they arrive back at that larger world, they must live by its logic, or at least that they cannot insert the logic of the smaller world into the larger. Gennarino perceives his mistake too late, sees it perhaps all in a flash in the image of his very unromantic wife. Now it is Raffaella's turn to choose. Naturally, Gennarino wants to return to the island, but, while *staying* might have had some plausibility, *going back* is clearly out of the question. Raffaella cannot bring herself to say no over the telephone—she can see Gennarino speaking to her from a gas station—but the decision is already written in her face: She must leave him. Something else is written there. If they should ever be brought together again on the yacht, she would certainly not treat him as she had before but neither could she love him as she did on the island. Both these forms of the relationship between man and woman are extremes. The ideal must lie somewhere in the middle, but what is it? St. Paul hardly knew what he said, and Raffaella does not even suspect it, that before God there is neither male nor female.

Raffaella is swept away by helicopter with her husband, and in a shot from her point of view Gennarino is left forever behind, to be swept away by his wife into the prison of his old world. For him, there is no vision of a third possibility; it is one prison or the other.

No doubt it is asking too much to find the *ideal* woman in the real world. In Wertmüller's view of the world one comes closest to the ideal with Tripolina and Salome (taken together) in *Love and Anarchy* and Fiore in *The Seduction of Mimi*.

As quoted earlier, Wertmüller says of Tripolina (Lina Polito) and Salome (Mariangela Melato) that they are very strong women who instinctively rebel against militarism and the patriarchal order. But their rebellion has different roots, as did their submission to the slavery of prostitution. Both, of course, sell their bodies as a means of livelihood, but with Tripolina one imagines it is only that, while with Salome it serves also as a base of operations for her political purposes. Salome's life as prostitute and anarchist began after she had witnessed the brutal slaying of her gentle lover by the Fascists, who had been singled out at random as the object of their attention after an assassination attempt at a political rally—singled out by the assassin himself to divert attention away from himself. Even though the anarchist's diversionary tactics are also to blame for her lover's death, it is only Fascism that merits Salome's hate; anarchy becomes her means of expressing it. Tripolina, on the other hand, is apolitical. She creates a small world out of a love that is basically instinctual with no reference to the larger world surrounding it. Where the hard-nosed Salome watches for prey like an eagle on a crag in the full glare of the sun, Tripolina, soft and sensual, sits like a quail in her hidden nest. It is the arrival of Tunin that brings her longing for love into open conflict with Salome's political will.

Tunin (Giancarlo Giannini) comes to the brothel in Rome in order to meet his contact, Salome; it is she who is supposed to arrange the details of Mussolini's assassination and Tunin's escape. In a sense they are kindred spirits: Like Salome, Tunin has been thrust into the political arena because of the murder of an older friend who happened to be an anarchist; but Tunin has none of Salome's strength. He is a timid soul with a brooding heart, and because he broods he can also burn; but instinctively he is drawn to Tripolina, in whose embrace he finds the warmth of the womb, a world against the world. The day comes when he must fulfill his mission. Tripolina is to wake him up at six in the morning. But at six o'clock she steps outside the room and forbids Salome to enter. Tunin shall not be awakened; he shall not be sent to his death. Love cries out in Tripolina: "What the hell is politics to us?" Anarchy in Salome answers: "Justice!" Love has the final word: "Justice, my ass. The dead are buried—that's justice!" Anarchy, wishing somehow to coexist with love, capitulates. Tunin shall not be awakened. But when Tunin wakes up to the sound of military music and realizes that his moment of mission has passed, he is like a man gone mad. Love and anarchy come together only to crush him, like the converging walls of the prison cell against which his head is smashed.

Love and anarchy (as an expression of will) are reconciled in Fiore, the sweater-knitting revolutionary of Turin in *The Seduction of Mimi*. Of all Wertmüller's women Fiore best represents, to date, the ideal. She is not a victim of the opposite sex nor of the society that the male sex has created: She is too independent and self-possessed for that. In no way can she be considered a tease, though Mimi in his sexual stupidity might consider her one when she refuses to yield to his passionate advances in the park. She claims to be, of all things, a virgin and intends to remain so until she can give herself to a man she really loves. For all her independence she is certainly not a ballbuster. Quite the contrary. While she has nothing but contempt for Mimi's vacillations, it is she who fills him for a time with self-respect, bringing both love and will to bear upon his character. When she leaves him at the end, it is because he has sacrificed love to machismo and surrendered his will to the old slavery. Fiore's love is not perfect; it has no social dimensions. "No sacrament," she says, "is going to stand in my way." The union that love effects needs no recognition except by the lovers themselves; the family it creates is never seen as part of a larger social fabric. Her will is not perfect either. Whose is? But when it expresses itself anarchistically, how effective an instrument is it really? One is reminded of Barzini's observation: "Only few Italians find solace in actual rebellion. Not all of the many members of the Communist Party want to start a revolution. Most of them want to enjoy the privileged status of revolutionaries in a frightened capitalist society."[14]

Still Fiore is the best of Wertmüller's women. She is better than all of Wertmüller's men.

III
Images of Man

There is a moment in the viewing of *Let's Talk About Men* when one is inclined to feel that Lina Wertmüller has revealed completely her impressions of men, if not of man. She calls it her feminist film, and it is certainly that. Released in 1965, just two years after the appearance of her first film, *The Lizards,*[1] it is a collection of four short satirical pieces, in black and white, cleverly held together by the humor of its framing situation.

A scholar (Nino Manfredi) with a fellowship from the Institute of Tropical Diseases is staying in the Roman apartment of a vacationing friend. While he showers, the water goes off. There is soap in his eyes and almost everywhere else. He leaves the apartment, naked, calling for the porter. The door closes, locking him out. The water of course goes back on. Voices drift up the stairs, so he hides in a broom closet. As he peeks through a crack in the door, a funeral procession proceeds down the stairs toward the street. "Some men cloak themselves with the outward signs of respectability," he hears one of the mourners say. The word is both a humorous comment on his plight and the stimulus for the first of his fantasies, entitled "A Man of Honor." Nino Manfredi plays the naked scholar as well as the men in each of the four episodes.

Federico, the man of honor, is a financial apprentice with an enterprising wife (Luciana Paluzzi). They live in an overstuffed, fluffy white apartment. Manuela's coy poses only barely conceal her cunning. Federico notices a string of pearls hanging from her bureau drawer. She will not tell her secret; his attempts to pry the drawer open are pure ineptitude. To overcome her boredom she has been stealing jewels for three years. He is appalled at her nonchalance; she has not even hidden them carefully.

They will be discovered, he insists, by the butler or the cat. Suppose the cat, a tom, were to appear with a necklace on, he conjectures. "Boys don't wear jewelry," she retorts. Turning to the predictable, if not static, world of men, Federico discovers on the phone with an associate that there has been a revolution in Syria. Panicked consultation over finances, all in the shadow of the Vatican, confirms his bankruptcy. Living in a garret with Manuela is out of the question; it would be "*La Boheme* by Zeffirelli," he muses. He could never get used to waiting for the communal toilet. Disguising his voice to sound like the butler's, he begins inviting wealthy friends and associates to a party. What the women will wear is, of course, extremely important. The attire will be formal. He cannot simply leave the stealing to his wife. Honor is a luxury one can easily discard in favor of a regular income.

Back on the stairs, the scholar leans over the railing to call for the janitor. Like the women of the episodes it doubtlessly symbolizes, the triangular stairwell has many levels. When women ascend the stairs, the exposed intellectual takes refuge in an elevator. Patients emerging from a doctor's office are instructed in the hazards of growing old. The subject of the second episode, "The Knife Thrower," is indeed an old man. Pedro and his wife, Saturnia (Milena Vukotic), a lifelong circus couple, are billed as the Infallible Morgas. Although Pedro claims forty years of triumph, Saturnia shows more than the usual signs of masculine fallibility. She has a wooden leg, the result of one of his poor aims in Ethiopia, and a patch over one eye from yet another miscalculation in Calabria. Pedro can brag even about his mistakes though: The chippendale table leg that replaces her own is, after all, a "beautiful carving," and the eye-patch earned her the title "The Pirate Queen," he boasts. Pedro wears glasses now, but Saturnia begs him to get new ones. It is not the glasses that matter; Saturnia is simply afraid, he insists. He threatens to abandon her for a younger associate, but we know—infallibly—that he could never survive without her scarred patience. He even insults her patron saint, who is appropriately enough St. Jude, the champion of hopeless cases. Love transforms her reverie. She sees Pedro as the handsome, competent knife-thrower he apparently never was and submits again to his practice. He aims with the knife; anguish seizes her face in anticipation. He pauses, cleans his glasses, and throws the knife. "How was that throw?" he demands. "Bad" is all she answers as she slips silently into death. "I've never missed with the second knife," he brags as if to bring her back to life. Then, with the pathetic bravado of a man who does not yet suspect the extent of his loss, he adds, "She pulls this on me at a time like this."

The naked professor rings the doorbell of a Marquessa's apartment and overhears a couple arguing about "A Superior Man," the type of the third episode. The first thing we note about the superior man is his inferior body. Raphael limps; a thick sole compensates for his shorter leg. His wife, Linda Lee (Margaret Lee), whom he calls derisively "my little Texas flower," is wearing a bottoms-out sailor suit. Although he claims that he detests her vulgar display of cheap sexuality, it is clear that she dresses to suit his perverted needs. She changes, but surely not for spite, into black stockings and a black negligee. Her reference to the "whip you used" is hint enough that sadomasochism is his game. She has been conditioned to be his victim. Raphael's continuous diatribe contrasts harshly with the serene Tibetan decor of their home. A Buddha observes their curious ritual. Because she has taken a lover, Linda Lee has tried to poison her husband, and he knows it. He easily detected the smell of bitter almond in his toothpaste. "A baboon," he taunts her, "makes fewer poor decisions." Killing him would have been easy; he proceeds to coax her. In the basement of their home, under the ominous arc of a swinging bat lamp, he dares her to kill him. Feigned death and a hoax killing are mere prelude to sex as they fall, kissing, into the grave he has prepared. The blood on his face is only cherry jam.

The frantic scholar, partially hidden from view by the railing, fails again in his search for help. The last of his imagined men brings us full circle back to reality and close to the core of Wertmüller's indictment of machismo. He is called simply "A Good Man," a title that carries opprobrium in inverse proportion to its modesty. The good man is all of the other men wrapped into one; he is both "superior" and "honorable," and even though he has not carved up his wife, he has nonetheless pinned her to a gibbet of servitude. She does not even seem to have a name. His, ironically, is Salvatore. She is the mother of four children; he is their father by insemination only. While he is still in bed, she has begun the day's work, singing. He complains: It is "a pain in the ass . . . to be awakened by singing." Before the "good" men are up in the morning, the women are washing their children's clothes. A child—for Salvatore—is the price one had to pay "for every night the bar wasn't open." Conception is, oddly enough, "a misfire."

The morning chores finished at home, the women begin working in the fields. Salvatore joins his cronies at the bar. There is work as usual in Don Cesare's olive groves. Don Fulgensio, the pastor, needs two men to clean a cellar. They are too busy to work; they will not leave the bar. Their aimless discussion continues. The only change in their occupation is to play cards. Not even a call to strike against Don Cesare and to sign up with the Communists interrupts their game. On the way home from the bar, Salvatore pauses with a companion in front of a billboard. It is no accident that Vittorio de Sica's *Ieri, oggi, domani (Yesterday, Today, Tomorrow)* is currently playing; Antonioni's *Red Desert* will begin the next day. The pattern of changeless days—past, present, and future—will yield a revolution, if anything at all. Salvatore returns home drunk; his wife is busy kneading dough. He complains about her weight, even calls her an "elephant," but demands his "rights" in bed once the lights are out. She protests in vain that she is too tired. Satisfied, he sleeps, while she returns to work. The "good man" is neither good nor a man; he is certainly no savior.

The film ends humorously where it begins, with the plight of the naked professor. The circular effect emphasizes the closed world of the dominant male. Back at his apartment, still without a key, he awaits the penalty of his unintentional exhibitionism. Water is pouring out from under the door; water and feet meet in a moment of visual irony, as urgent voices rise up the stairwell. "He's naked, . . . he's dangerous," they warn. The police will arrive momentarily.

There is a sense finally in which the credits at the beginning say it all. A divided screen provides credits on the right while showing in the left half a succession of "real" men—comically dated pictures of muscle men, one balancing a column, another holding a baby, and military men in a variety of inane outfits. No one of the men portrayed in detail in the film is a whole man; they are scarcely even halves. If one is tempted to see the episodes as presenting discreet types, on reflection the discrimination dissolves mostly into narrative. Mostly. The first three men—the man of honor, the knife-thrower, and the superior man—are potentially good men. There is an ironic progression though toward evil. The good man is clearly the worst of all.

Male types emerge with greater clarity in Wertmüller's films of the seventies. One clear image of man in the more recent films that is at best foreshadowed in *Let's Talk About Men* is the *man with a cause*. Perhaps the knife-thrower is a symbolic suggestion of this later development; he certainly typifies the folly of the idealist in Wertmüller's world. To be a political assassin, she says, is like a blind man throwing knives. In the end, like the knife-thrower, the assassin is hurt the most by the failure of his death-defying act. Men with a cause are Wertmüller's anarchists, Tunin in *Love and Anarchy* and Pedro in *Seven Beauties*. The order that tyrants impose is inexorably stronger than the isolated efforts of the assassin. However much Wertmüller despises rigidly imposed order (the images are compelling—the cold sterility of the square, like a de Chirico painting, awaiting the arrival of Mussolini in *Love and Anarchy* and Pedro's preferring to "die in shit" rather than live under Fascism in *Seven Beauties*), she will not allow herself the ultimate folly of denying the superiority of force and numbers.

Tunin in *Love and Anarchy,* after watching the Fascists kill an admired older friend (or perhaps a teacher, we never know the exact nature of the relationship), sets out to assassinate Mussolini. His resolve is uneducated; its intensity, monomaniacal. It pierces through the mist in his eyes. Tunin is just a simple peasant; his freckled face is soft and innocent. The lush green countryside of his origin warns us that he is altogether unequal to the task. When Tunin as a child had asked his mother what an anarchist was, her answer became tragic prediction: "Someone who kills a prince or a king and is hanged for it."

Love and Anarchy, like its title, is a film of contrasts, abstract and real, symbolic and natural. The verdant marshes oppose the amber warmth of the whorehouse where Tunin contacts the anarchist Salome, who is to help him with the details of his mission. (Fascists, murdering her lover, had driven her to prostitution.) Spatoletti (Eros Pagni), chief of Mussolini's security police, is a customer of Salome's; he is the witless source of her information about Mussolini's public appearances. He is pure bombast, a base sycophant. In one crass image he demonstrates the emptiness of fascist tyranny and sexist domination. Mussolini, he boasts, "has a pair of balls big enough to screw the whole world."

Nothing apparently can shake Tunin from his purpose; not even love can save him. When he falls in love with Tripolina, another prostitute, we are drawn to him enough to hope against hope. Finally she persuades Salome not to awaken him on the morning of the planned assassination, but Tunin's fate is set. To awaken him is to send him to certain death; but so is not to awaken him, as it turns out. His plans thwarted, Tunin goes berserk, shooting mere soldiers in an empty act of frustrated defiance. Spatoletti demands to know who he is. "Nobody" is Tunin's honest, manly answer. His captors smash his head against a stone wall. His heart after all had been clearer than his head. The heart had made the man; it was the cause that took his life.

Wertmüller's most explicit (and least artistic) declaration of attitude toward political assassination comes at the end of the film where she permits herself this direct quotation from the Italian anarchist Enrico Malatesta: "I would like to stress again the horror I feel towards assassinations. Aside from being evil acts in themselves, they are foolish acts, for they harm the very cause they were to serve. However, these assassins could truly be regarded as saints as well as heroes, but only when their brutal action and the passion that misled them are forgotten and the things remembered will be their martyrdom and the ideal that inspired them." Tunin's attempt at assassination is a miserable failure: He can be neither saint nor hero. But, the insanity of anarchy aside, Tunin is at least a man—with a cause—and Wertmüller treats him with dignity appropriate to his setting.

The image of man that predominates in Wertmüller's films is not however the man with a cause, but rather the *macho with a cause*. Whereas the former is clearly an idealist, the latter is simply confused. His cause, such as it is, is quickly lost in a reversion to machismo. Carletto in *All Screwed Up* falls somewhere between these two types. Although he is by far the most developed male character in the film, his cause—a quixotic challenge of the urban industrial establishment—is somehow lost in the film's overall emphasis on the screwed-up city itself. His frustrated idealism is swept up into the pure visual metaphor of circular frenzy; what death there is for his cause is symbolized by the realization that his energy has been wasted by an imprisoning system. If his cause is not man-sized, neither is his youth corrupted by a tradition of empty honor. His defeat is at least honest.

Gennarino in *Swept Away* and Mimi in *The Seduction of Mimi* are the real machos with causes. As long as Gennarino is the victimized sailor on the yacht serving Raffaela and her friends, all seems to be right, except of course to Gennarino. At least the lines are clear: He belongs to the communist masses subjugated by the capitalist few. There seems to be little chance that "the garden of Europe," as Raffaela puts it, "will be turned into a concrete anthill for the masses of Europe"—with Raffaela in the ascendancy. Gennarino's bitter anticapitalist mutterings are certainly understandable. Yet his T-shirts are dirty and malodorous; the coffee he serves is cold, and the pasta is thick. There is some truth therefore to Raffaela's calling him a "typical grunty Southern slob," but it has nothing to do with ideology.

Stranded with Raffaela by that most "unusual destiny" on a Mediterranean island,[2] Gennarino continues to mouth proletarian invective. "Social democrat whore," he calls her. Yet his behavior is pure male chauvinism. In justification of his brutality, he simply claims, "I'm doing what the rich do." He demands to be called "Mr. Carrunchio." When he insists that "women were meant to serve men," he has abandoned Marx and returned to the worst of St. Paul. Once again he trades politics for sexist struggle. He awaits nothing more than the moment Raffaela will address him, "Sir—my lord—my master." The only two lessons he acknowledges as such are these: "Money doesn't count here, *you* have to work" (the emphasis is perhaps redundant), and "Stop insulting me." His real lesson seems to be "You've got to love me; I've got to become your god!" He commands, "Kiss my hand." Raffaela later voluntarily kisses even his foot. So complete is her sexist victimization, he is no longer simply a "specimen of Mediterranean manhood." "You are man as he should have been in nature before everything changed," she proclaims. Somehow the revolutionary implications of his "You're going to pay for everybody" before they make love is lost completely afterwards when he brags, "Never did I see you look so satisfied when you were on the yacht." Ineffectual too is his protest against the garland she lays on his groin. He labels it the "plaything of the idle rich," but clearly elicits the phallic homage. When he agrees to sodomize her (he is ignorant of the word, of course, but not the reality), she calls him her "first real man."

As the rescue boat appears on the horizon, the camera zooms abruptly to Gennarino in a tree, Raffaela on the beach. The moment of truth has arrived. She wants to run and hide, because she knows that the world will (and must) change them. Equally unrealistic is his preference for rescue: He insists that she prove her love, that she choose him over wealth and power. Back on the mainland he plots their return to the island. The *Santa Rosalia,* named for his patron saint, is to take them back. Surrounded again by her husband and wealthy friends, she is nothing but a mirage. Gennarino sends flowers and a ring, purchased with the money he has won as reward. He observes her from a distance, content till the very end that she at least surely knows "Gennarino Carrunchio." A plaintive aria erupts on the sound track as Gennarino receives her note of denial. Ascending with Raffaela in the helicopter, the camera observes an ever-diminishing Gennarino as he runs to the end of the jetty. With Raffaela swept away to Milan, Gennarino is left below to contend with a ballbusting wife, who quickly gets him in tow. "One bitch up there, one down here, and my friend the sea a traitor," he grumbles, but follows his wife along the wharf, carrying her bag. Wertmüller disdains a melodramatic ending in favor of the harsh but simple reality of the macho in chains despite himself. His proletarian cause has been swept away not only on the blue sea of August, but also in the air and on land. It is the unusual though expected destiny of one who dares pit private phallus against public wealth.

Although the American title *The Seduction of Mimi* is more pleasing aesthetically and happier actually on all counts, the more direct Italian title *Mimi, Metalworker, Wounded in Honor* gives emphatic position to the source of Mimi's downfall—his southern manhood's double standard of honor. It also alludes to the occasion of his short-lived cause, his employment in Turin as a metalworker. *The Seduction of Mimi*, Wertmüller's third film and the first to be released in the seventies, is a structurally precise film in which form (here setting) and meaning are close to perfectly balanced. Its visual symmetry is second only to *Seven Beauties.*

As we have already seen, it begins and ends with a sound-car dispensing Mafia propaganda in a rock quarry. Midway in the film, the revelation that shapes Mimi's fate is made in a car in the quarry. It begins and ends in Catania, Sicily, the southern source and cause of Mimi's wounded "honor." Between beginning and ending, though certainly without rigid temporal division, is Mimi's northern interlude as communist metalworker in Turin, the place of his union of love with Fiore. In Catania there are unions only of tradition and revenge.

Wertmüller also uses to full comic effect the repetition of visual and sound devices. Mimi's full name is Carmelo Mordocheo. Three times he is summoned by name in imperious tones from offscreen, and each of these times he turns to discover that he is being addressed by a different man with three moles on his right cheek. Three other times the camera zooms in at crucial moments to reveal the distinctive triangle of moles. The voice off frame in its threefold repetition has a biblical explanation. Samuel in the service of Eli had to be summoned by the

Lord three times before he accepted his prophetic mission (I Sam. 3:1-10). Whether or not Wertmüller had this precise biblical allusion in mind is immaterial. The imperious manner in which the voice interrupts the action off frame clearly suggests—what certainly seems to be Mimi's growing fear— that his fate is being dictated by some potent external force. It cannot be "the persecution of a ubiquitous and omnipotent Mafia chieftain"[3] that Peter Biskind has Mimi discern and other critics noted. Only four of the six men with moles are obviously Mafiosi. The cardinal, at the end of the film, could of course be Mafia-related as well as the comrade at the communist meeting in Turin, early in the film, but the affiliation of these latter two ought more simply to be found in other symbols of the establishment—church and party. If one discounts his use of the singular, Biskind seems to be on surer ground when he assesses the psychological function of the apparitions of moles. "Although the ontological status of this figure is unclear (there *is* an exploiting class in the film for which he seems to stand)," he writes, "it is evident that Mimi's delusions of persecution are an externalization of his own voluntary but unexamined choices."[4] That Mimi's basic problem stems from his own projections onto reality rather than his accurate reading of it seems only too clear.

The film opens with a view of the rock quarry in Catania from inside the Mafia sound car. The workers are being "urged" to vote for the Mafia candidate; all the while they are assured that the ballot will be completely secret. Mimi (Giancarlo Giannini), with the kind of vincible stupidity that characterizes his every major move, scoffs at the notion of a secret ballot—"They [the Mafia] know the number of hairs on your ass," he observes without finesse but with clarity—yet votes for the Communist candidate anyway. The day after the election he is fired from his job. It is Don Calogero of the Sicilian Brotherhood whose voice is heard offscreen and who announces Mimi's dismissal. His political quandary parallels his sexual frustration. His wife Rosalia (Agostina Belli) is physically reticent, if not frigid, perhaps because the portraits of her parents preside over their sexual fumblings from the wall behind the bed. "If we don't have children," Mimi grumbles, "it's your fault." Then, in desperation, he asks her for some sign of life. "Pant, speak, do something," he pleads.

Once in Turin, employed as a metalworker, Mimi learns quickly the worker's way of survival in the north; he joins the union and the party. Politics, Mimi is assured, is "something with you all day long." Even buying a pair of pants has political implications. At a party meeting, Mimi once again hears the peremptory summons, "Carmelo Mordocheo." The speaker with moles is a party comrade. "Fear," the comrade explains, "is like a drug; it makes you see things that aren't there." As the film's story unfolds, we will come to wonder whether fear is perhaps Mimi's worst enemy, worse even than honor.

Fiore (Mariangela Melato), whom Mimi observes working contentedly on a boulevard island, is already a dedicated radical. At a makeshift kiosk she sells sweaters and distributes revolutionary literature; there are posters of Che, Marx, and Mao. Mimi, at a distance, sees only Fiore. In the film's most beautiful sequence, Mimi moves even closer to the love he has fallen for. They stroll across a hazy winter landscape, one of Turin's parks; there is an aria from *La Traviata* and no dialogue. Fiore is not easily won, but Mimi experiences the beginnings of a love he has never known with Rosalia. Wertmüller, the realist, will not give us pure romance; comedy interrupts Mimi's courtship. He wrestles Fiore to the ground, but she defends herself effectively. "It wasn't rape," he apologizes, "it was passion." She protests that she is a virgin; he asks incredulously, "Your zodiac sign?" Only for love, she insists, will she surrender her body. Succumbing finally to his entreaties, she sets the condition for their living together: "If you ever dare touch another woman, even your wife, I'll leave you." Their love skirts reality as their movement along a road traces an arc through the park.

Wertmüller's sense of visual parallelism provides the continuity between Catania and Turin, between bed with Rosalia and love with Fiore. There is some evidence of Mimi's initial impotence with Fiore, perhaps because she too has portraits hanging on the wall above her bed—not of natural parents, but ideological.⁵ Marx and Engels behind the bed intimidate Mimi only slightly; Lenin peers from a commanding position elsewhere in Fiore's spacious garret room. Mimi's cause, at this time so fresh, will of course never supplant virility as the source of his drive. The sunburst window above the portraits over the bed contributes ironically to the aura of genesis in their shared lodging. "I'll massacre you with love," Mimi promises. It is not revolution, or necessarily even lasting love, that is born here for certain—only a child. Mimi corresponds with Rosalia, who sends news of her "liberation." With Fiore still in bed, Mimi reads Rosalia's letter; as he reads, the film cuts to Catania. Rosalia rides to work in a steam laundry on a newly purchased motor bike: "With due precautions," she assures him. The precautions seem limited to stickers of the Sacred Heart and Blessed Virgin on the bike's shaft. Mimi curses the fact that Rosalia is "already a member of consumer society."

The year's interlude in Turin comes to an abrupt ending. During a champagne christening party for their son, Mimi stumbles unhappily upon a Mafia massacre. Five bodies litter the floor; one is Mimi's, feigning death. Mimi only barely avoids being included in the number of Don Tricarico's enemies. The Don of course has three moles on his right cheek. Preserved as a potentially dangerous witness, Mimi hears the summons, from offscreen, for the third and last time. His lordship, the chief of police, has the moles too. Frightened by the mounting evidence of collusion, Mimi babbles, "I'm sorry. I can't help you. I don't know anything." The penalty Mimi must pay for being a reluctant witness is deportation back home to be watched. At the foundry, he is told that his "request for a transfer" has been granted; he has been assigned as foreman to the factory in Catania. Mimi's protest—"I didn't request it"—is obviously ineffectual. The "holy family," in hilarious disguise, sneaks into the "promised land" in a car sagging with baggage. Fiore is clearly a comic Madonna. Getting his second wife and only child—so far—hidden away in Catania is of course no easy feat.

The general manager of the factory in Catania, with moles of course, instructs a bristling, but eventually submissive Mimi. "My cousin Salvatore Tricarico in Turin wants me to look after you" establishes the Mafia connection. "Politicians," he explains to Mimi, "put things in order." Then, in an isolated moment of apparent self-determination, Mimi flouts the Brotherhood; what is even more important, he seems to realize—if only briefly—that he can shape his own fate. When the general manager doubles over in a fit of coughing, Mimi seems to see him not as a symbol of power but merely as a feeble old man, and in a gesture of contempt throws back the few lire that the Don had made him grovel for; then he turns abruptly and strides past the immobile bodyguards. Nevertheless, the old Mimi reappears shortly thereafter; he effectively becomes a mouthpiece for the system when he opposes the possibility of a strike. "There must be order," he tells the workers, "enough of so-called progress."

Dividing his time between Fiore in hiding and Rosalia at home, Mimi must plead "exhaustion" to the latter, now unexpectedly aggressive in bed. Mimi quickly discovers, with total offense to his southern manhood, that he is being called "queer" for his inability to perform with Rosalia. In a car in the rock quarry, his cousins tell him the news about Rosalia. She is already pregnant; they and Mimi know of course that it is not by him. Enraged, he attacks Rosalia with kung-fu blows. Draped in a black shawl as if mourning for her virtue, she dodges his wrath, but makes her confession. While getting her driver's license, she chatted—too long—with a sergeant in the customs police. Her self-righteous description assumes without warrant the modesty of the *Inferno*'s Paolo and Francesca episode. Amilcare Finochiarro, the father of five children, had taken her once in the cabin of a crane. Mimi accuses her of making him out to be a queer; then in defense of his manhood, he confesses the presence of Fiore and his child, and the order of expressed wrath is reversed: Rosalia descends on him like a Fury.

At first he resists help from the Brotherhood in preserving his honor. Exposing his double standard of fidelity, Mimi plots alone an appropriate revenge against the customs officer. Peppino, the contact, is forever lurking, waiting. Mimi will seduce Finochiarro's grotesquely obese wife Amalia (Elena Fiore) and impregnate her. He dogs her steps until she agrees to meet him in the Church of St. Nicholas, a fitting spot for an assignation that will lead to his intended gift since the Christian imagination readily associates St. Nick with the birth of a child. He assuages her fear; their meeting in another kind of cabin, one by the sea, will be purely for platonic reasons, he insists. They tango, then tangle, but not until Mimi overcomes her initial considerable resistance. Then Amalia, obsessed by the thought that she could be as sexually attractive to Mimi as he claims, finally connives her own revenge against Amilcare, who caught her "by a trick." He got her pregnant so she had to marry him; she will join Mimi's plan from "duty not pleasure." Wertmüller resorts to visual repetition and lens distortion, as we have noted, to stress both the physical immensity of Amalia and the enormity of Mimi's revulsion for his sexual chore. Three times we see the same view, from behind of course, of Amalia taking off her pants; twice her attempt at a seductive over-the-shoulder glance. When Amalia crawls to Mimi across the bed, she is literally all behind; the distorted lens makes it fill the screen. When the camera assumes Mimi's perspective, her huge breasts are like inverted mountains of flesh crushing his body. Whereas Finochiarro was apparently a onetime winner, Mimi and Amalia need months of carefully charted vaginal temperatures to score. Mimi even has trouble proving his enemy a cuckold.

The final act of the plot of revenge, for which Mimi accepts the assistance of the Mafia, is pure mock opera. Mimi challenges Finochiarro to meet him on the steps of the church to swap babies (in Mimi's mind evidently the father alone is parent of the child) in hopes that he can taunt the sergeant into attempted murder. The confrontation before the assembled crowd goes as planned—with one fatal exception. After Peppino, hidden in the mob, kills the cornered officer, he puts the gun in Mimi's hand and flees. At the point of maximum confusion, a cardinal and his secretaries emerge from a car on an elevated roadway to behold the spectacle. The camera zooms in to capture the expression of horror on his face for the desecration of a sacred place; what we actually see is the triangle of moles on his cheek. Mimi goes to jail, the apparent victim of Catania's "system"—the Brotherhood. He is actually the victim of his own double standard.

Pardoned by the Don, Mimi is released from prison, only to be swarmed by another kind of mob—his dependents. His women and their children converge from all sides, Rosalia and Fiore with one apiece, Amalia with six. Even in the battle of children, the dead Finochiarro has bested Mimi six to two. To support them, Mimi decides to do anything the Mafia asks. Where his seduction began, there it is complete. He had been seduced first into thinking that his vote was secret; now, in the sound-car back at the quarry, he solicits votes for Don Tricarico. Fiore approaches in a red van, brightly decorated with hammer and sickle, faithful finally to her revolutionary cause, not Mimi, whom she intends to leave. He pleads with her to remain, thinking foolishly that "They're my cousins, all of them" will satisfy Fiore as an explanation of his complete capitulation to the Brotherhood.

Mimi's abandonment, like Gennarino's in *Swept Away*, is from the woman's perspective although there is little comparison, as we have noted, in the women. Mimi tries to run after the van. A trucking shot from the van shows the desperation of Mimi's pursuit; a long shot from a crane gives us van, runner, and the expanse of the quarry. Once again there is a trucking shot from the van of Mimi losing ground; then finally from afar, the camera zooms in on the exhausted, isolated macho, a bug crawling in the dust of the quarry. If he is the victim of the Brotherhood, it is because its values and his are fundamentally the same. The ruthless defense of name and honor subverts individual *and* society. Mimi, like Wertmüller's other machos with a cause, abandons common cause for the security of personal phallic power.

In the terms of *Let's Talk About Men,* all of Wertmüller's later machos, with or without causes, are "men of honor"; it is this empty title that the macho is fated to defend by whatever means in his power. Her machos with a cause, Gennarino and Mimi, are "superior men," whereas the *mere macho,* the macho without a cause—Pasqualino—is the "good man" come to frightening term.

Seven Beauties (Pasqualino Settebellezze in Italian) is divided into seven sequences, four in the present time of the film, three intercut within as flashbacks illuminating the present. The number seven, both in the title and in the structure of sequences, yields meaning on several levels. "Seven Beauties" *(Settebellezze)* is Pasqualino's nickname; his family name is Frafuso. Pasqualino has seven sisters, who are anything but beauties. He admits that he is ugly, but that "women love him"; and so the word has gotten around, he claims, that "he must have the seven beauties." It is doubtlessly a nickname of utter contrast since it involves seven, the number of completion or perfection. Wertmüller is of course aware of the implications of the title. In an interview the spring *Seven Beauties* was released in the United States (1976), she talked about symbolism and implicitly about the depths of irony she was working with in the film: "The number seven is a number full of implication. In many medieval sayings they give the number seven as the number of perfection. When you say, 'A perfect person,' it's seven beauties that make a perfect person!"[6]

Structurally, too, the film's seven sequences suggest completion or, by extension of the same concept, enclosure. "Man *is* society, man's actions are profoundly tied up with the society that produced him, and society is the product of the same man," she said in the same interview. "So this theme is like a circle, and it eats it own tail!"[7] Actually, the film's structure is doubly closed inasmuch as the three episodes from the past are enclosed within the four in time present; one of the principal reasons why the number seven was considered the most perfect is that it is the sum of the two primary numbers of completion, three and four.

One final implication of the title, that Wertmüller did not mention explicitly but is undoubtedly aware of, arises from the fact that the number seven is the fundamental structural unit of the Book of Revelation. *Seven Beauties* is indeed apocalyptic, both as ultimate revelation and as catastrophe. It reveals the depths of human perversity that make holocaust inevitable.

The film begins with an introductory montage of Fascist and Nazi documentary war footage at perfect counterpoint in its seriousness to the satirical song "Oh Yeah" that accompanies it. The verses of the song, each ending with the caustic "Oh Yeah," actually provide astute political commentary on the whole film. Hitler and Mussolini shake hands, smile and grin, offer gestures of support to the people, intercut with slow motion scenes of exploding shells, strafing, destruction, and death, as the singer wryly observes:

> The ones who should have been shot in the cradle . . . Pow! Oh yeah!
> The ones who say follow me to success, but kill me if I fail, so to speak, Oh yeah!
> The ones who say we Italians are the greatest he-men on earth, Oh yeah! . . .
> The ones who say be calm, be calm, Oh yeah! . . .
> The ones who believe Christ is Santa Claus as a young man, Oh yeah! . . .
> The ones who keep going, keep going, just to see how it all ends, Oh yeah! . . .
> The ones who lose wars by the skin of their teeth, Oh yeah![8]

Carefully edited into the concluding newsreel shots are images in grainy-textured print of a bandaged figure slipping out of a boxcar in the night. It is Pasqualino (Giancarlo Giannini) deserting the Fascist army; his wounds are feigned. He and his fellow deserter Francesco (Piero di Orio) are somewhere in Germany, a rain forest near the Rhine perhaps. "How can you trust people," Pasqualino curses, "who send you out in cardboard shoes? When you blow your nose, you get a crystal chandelier. When you shit, you get icicles." The discarded bandages had helped at least to keep him warm.

Off in the hazy distance of the valley, they see some sign of movement. Cautious, they stop to watch. Men, women, and children—all Jews—are being lined up on a hillside, gunned down, and prepared casually for mass graves by Nazi soldiers. "We're in it as deep as these men too," Francesco reflects. "You mean we're just like them?" Pasqualino asks, without genuine insight, just enough perception to convert Francesco's statement into a question. Francesco, building an image of the true man, continues to reflect aloud, "In the face of certain things, you've got to say No." The sight of murder has opened the passages of Pasqualino's memory: "I killed for a woman before the war," he admits. It is a superficial association of images—for him. For the viewer, the horrendous link between cosmic holocaust and petty honor is first forged; through visual parallel and narrative irony, past and present will be welded together in an unbreakable chain of insight. The first episode in the present ends; the camera pans up the trunks of the giant trees in a swirl that fades easily into a matching pan up the huge churning thighs of a cheap burlesque dancer, Pasqualino's sister.

Concettina (Elena Fiore), dressed scantily but patriotically in red-white-and-green garter and girdle, struts and shuffles up and down the stage; the bouncing rhythm of her vaudeville number is ludicrous tease. The reaction from her patrons is mockery rather than delight. A man enters the back of the hall; we see only his feet, descending in rhythm with the music, against the thin red lights on the stairs. The camera pans up the man; it is a slightly younger, certainly cleaner Pasqualino, present to defend the honor of his family and his sister from insult. In her dressing room, Pasqualino tries to shout sense into Concettina. A richly layered shot shows Pasqualino, threatening Concettina, their reflections in her mirror, and behind them the distant image of the mannequin-clown who has taken the stage. Both Pasqualino and Concettina fuse into the mannequin because each is manipulated though in different ways, Concettina by Pasqualino and Totonno, her reputed "lover" (actually just a pimp-manager), Pasqualino by the Mafia's prevailing masculine ethic of honor and dignity. Let Totonno be warned, Pasqualino threatens; Concettina lies to her brother that Totonno has promised marriage. As Pasqualino leaves his sister's dressing room, the deep focus is from the stage, with the clown dominant, Pasqualino on the stairs, and Concettina in the rear, distraught and sobbing. The shift in view only serves to emphasize the pitiful limits of their freedom.

Considering Concettina's condition, we are no doubt expected to conclude that she is lucky to find work somehow. The alternative is scarcely appealing. The family lives in and operates a small, primitive mattress factory; Pasqualino oversees the "enterprise" from his self-appointed perch. While his mother and sisters, in cramped quarters, stuff the mattresses, he preens before a mirror, slicks down his hair, cocks his hat at the proper angle, tucks a gun securely in his belt ("I have to defend our honor," he boasts, "it's all we have; the pistol means respect"), delivers brief exhortations to the slaving women, pats behinds for encouragement's sake, and swaggers out into the streets of Naples. Pasqualino's stroll down a narrow street, under the adoring gaze of women, is a masterpiece of cocky self-contentment and groundless pretension. Enzo Iannaci's brilliant score complements perfectly the visual panache of the scene. From an overview of the Bay of Naples, Pasqualino tries to cheer up a young girl (Francesca Marciano), a street-singer with a parrot. "Why the tears?" he queries. "Ask your parrot to tell my fortune." "I don't want to sing," she protests, "I have no voice." With the urgency of the messiah for all, he utters a few reassuring, saving words: "Just worry about growing up." And, then, before passing on, "If anyone bothers you, just tell them you're engaged to Pasqualino." He leaves her, sweet and innocent—for now—while disclosing the pathetic source of the only salvation he can offer, the shield of his manhood.

In Naples' Gothic, glass-enclosed concourse, Pasqualino encounters Don Raffaele (Enzo Vitale), the Mafia boss. It is a shame, he warns, "when a man's family isn't respected." The conversation is typically muted counsel against dishonor; its implications are obvious. Pasqualino has been deceived by his sister. Storming into the bordello, where her promise of "marriage" to Totonno is being fulfilled, Pasqualino assaults his sister and is instantly pounced upon by the other prostitutes, eager to come to Concettina's defense. "Eighteen Karats" Totonno (Mario Conti) and his henchmen appear with apocalyptic suddenness, frozen in judgment on the stairs leading into the hall. Pasqualino, cautiously, challenges Totonno; but the latter is clearly in command. In the brilliantly edited sequel, quickly paced with exaggerated camera angles, Totonno scornfully calls Pasqualino "You ugly little worm" and knocks him unconscious. The camera catches his quick departure, from the floor behind Pasqualino's inert form.

This first episode from the past ends as anticipated, with the murder Pasqualino had confessed to Francesco. In the dead of night, Pasqualino moves through the streets toward Totonno's quarters, past a stained-glass Virgin and Child in the tower of a church. Wertmüller's eye leaves no irony, no detail undiscovered. Letting himself quietly into Totonno's room, the brave Pasqualino takes aim at his sleeping victim. Squeezing the trigger seems only to produce sweat on his brow. Then, the gun fires, unexpectedly, clearly (from the consternation on Pasqualino's face) before he had intended to shoot, if indeed he were man enough to have done it intentionally. Totonno lies dead. The return of Concettina's music covers the cut back to the German forest.

In their efforts to avoid capture by the Nazis, Pasqualino and Francesco are close to starving. Like a mirage a German country home appears in the distance, nestled in lush green foliage. A woman's voice can be heard singing Wagner's *"Träume"* ("Dreams"). The camera pans the Baroque opulence of the house, tracking with Pasqualino till the right window will disclose the singer. A half-naked woman sits upright at the piano, as unaware of the glaring eyes of Pasqualino as she apparently is of the war being waged around her. Pasqualino is starved more for food than sex, however. An old woman sits at the end of a kitchen table laden with food; Pasqualino grabs sausage, cheese, and bread, muttering reassurance and compliments in butchered German. He leaves hastily, so thrilled with his prize that he loses his way. An adroit, continuous, long shot of his departure through the door, taken from the viewpoint of the silent, immovable crone, shows Pasqualino dart first right, then left, before heading straight off into the distance. The feast with Francesco is cut short—in mid-bite in fact—by the sudden, frightening appearance of towering Nazi soldiers.

The concentration camp they are sent to is a horrifying visualization of the circles of Dante's hell, but the horror of this hell reflects not the crime of its victims but the mind of their oppressors. Its bleak atmosphere is presented to the violent strains of Wagner's "The Ride of the Valkyries," the opposite pole of the German spirit from the still lingering sentimentality of *"Träume."* Dead bodies lie in piles, hang from rafters; other standing, breathing, emaciated hulks, grey as corpses, house souls soon to depart. The descent of vast hordes down the stairs, the peering presence of others crammed into cavelike cells, is pure *Inferno,* its masterful evocation linking Wertmüller's imagination with Italy's unrivaled heritage of art. The only touch of irony in a passage of total realism, itself perhaps a remembered irony, comes as two prisoners wander among the corpses, playing a waltz on their violins.[9]

Pasqualino's question "How did the world get like this?" though clearly beyond the range of his capacity for answers, does not however go unanswered. Dead center to the theme of *Seven Beauties,* it is the question the film addresses in the manner of art. Pasqualino, as always, is on surer ground when he expresses his own inner urges. "I like being alive," he tells Francesco and their fellow prisoner Pedro (Fernando Rey). His plan of survival focuses directly on the camp's grotesque commandant (Shirley Stoler), modeled apparently on Ilse Koch, the notorious wife of the infamous commander of Büchenwald. Her head is like a globe whose axis is evil itself. Pasqualino stares at the commandant, remembering his mother's song about even the wickedest woman in the world having a little bit of sweetness in her. The cut is to a woman singing to her child. Getting to that woman's heart is like drinking coffee, bitter on top, but sweet on the bottom; it has to be stirred to bring the sugar to one's lips. The prisoners in line for inspection, Pasqualino hums as the commandant passes. "She's got to have that little bit of sugar," he hears his mother say; "no matter how rotten she is, she needs love." Pasqualino's appropriation of the lullaby is characteristically and dangerously facile; no matter how bleak man's plight, his penis will suffice.

Back in their cells, Pedro the anarchist dominates the scene. "I'm a death expert, an anarchist who failed," he confesses to his friends. He had made attempts on the lives of Hitler, Mussolini, and Salazar. "And they've made death an industry," he acknowledges with regret. Responding to Pasqualino's "I want to live, I want to have children, and see my children's children, and my children's children's children," Pedro predicts a starving, overpopulated world where "whole families will be slaughtered for an apple." "Too bad," he laments, in an expression of hope that is at the core of his and Wertmüller's mythic claims, "because I believe in man, but in a new man that must be born, a civilized man, not that intelligent man who has tilted nature's balance and destroyed everything, a new man who can rediscover harmony within himself." "Put things in order?" Pasqualino asks. "Oh, no," Pedro pleads, "the Germans are orderly. No, man in disorder . . . that's the only hope . . . man in disorder."

There is of course no creative disorder in the episode from the past that follows, only a parody of the order that makes corpses of the living. The flashback is to Pasqualino killing Totonno, surprise and fear etched into his face. He goes directly to the source. Don Raffaele's office resembles a room in the Galleria Borghesi; a puny Don counsels creative disposal of the corpse as heroic Heracles struggles with a centaur. The myth of *onore solo* replaces the age of the gods. Don Raffaele reminds Pasqualino of the varieties of imaginative interment his Neapolitan brothers have been justly famous for, and we see in succession a comic repetition of the horrors of the concentration camp: sea burial with a rock anchor, extra bodies in the coffin, and fresh skeletons in the Old Bone House of Naples. Honor made Pasqualino a murderer; imagination will get him into jail. He decides on dismemberment; he will ship Totonno in three parts as provolone to Palermo, Milan, and Genoa. The plan is easier made than executed. Just getting the heavy Totonno from the bed to the table for sawing is exhaustion enough for Pasqualino. He falls under the weight of the body, slides under the table in a tub of sand, hits his head, guzzles wine, as Totonno continues to snore and fart. The orifices of the dead are evidently as hard to silence as those of the living. He lowers the suitcases to the street from a high window; the camera deftly matches the jerks of the descending bags.[10] A blind man's dog, sniffing their contents, harasses Pasqualino as he departs by carriage for the depot; porters try in vain to help him unload. His proud announcement to Don Raffaele by phone that the shipments are on their way jump cuts to his humiliating flight from home as Concettina, screaming "Murderer," leads the police in to get him. A frantic chase along rooftops and a leap across a passageway to another building, while providing escape from one group of pursuers, delivers Pasqualino safely into the arms of another detachment of police. Apprehension in Naples cuts to punishment in the concentration camp.

Pasqualino breaks ranks and follows the commandant, behind walls, beneath a sign reading *"Aborte"* (German for toilets), softly crooning his silly love song. For punishment he must stand at attention alone in the middle of the assembly hall, with his hands behind his head. A far shot shows the expanse of the hall, the isolated figure painfully struggling to remain erect, and the commandant circling him, stuffed into the sidecar of a motorcycle. Invariably photographed to maximum effect, the concentration camp displays, ironically enough, classical dimensions. John Simon reports that it was Enrico Job who found the location with the aid of an assistant. After visiting Germany, Yugoslavia, and Rumania, they decided upon an abandoned paper factory, built over the foundation of an ancient temple of Jupiter, just twelve miles from Rome at Tivoli.[11]

The vigorous rhythm of dance music signals the return to Naples and the past. Pasqualino, proclaimed the "Hatchet Killer," confesses his crime. "I did it as an act of honor," he explains in his defense. His lawyer (Lucio Amelio), appalled, warns him, "It's your life or your honor." As base as Pasqualino's concept of honor is, we have more than an inkling already which one he will choose. The lawyer insists that they will have to plead insanity. When he is allowed to see his family, he asks his mother (Ermelinad de Felice) how they can afford the lawyer. She shrugs as if to say "Don't ask" or "We manage somehow," equivalently admitting that Concettina's profession has spread to the other girls, at least. In the prison yard, Pasqualino, in support of the plea of insanity, imitates Mussolini, strutting, swaggering, declaiming. He is carried off shouting about "a race of artists and warriors that challenge the world."

It was a stroke of genius to film the trial completely in pantomime; for what is inevitably an excess of words becomes, under Wertmüller's astute direction and the unfailing eye of her cinematographer, Tonino delli Colli, a beautifully controlled but doubly expressive battle of glances. Everyone of any importance—to Pasqualino—is there: his mother, his seven sisters, now all blondes, the young street-singer whom Pasqualino had encouraged, the lawyer, and of course Don Raffaele. Except for the movement of eyes, the people lining the stalls could be frescoes matching those on the walls. The camera dwells for a moment on an ostrich—a symbol of ignored reality—in one of the paintings. The courtroom is a gem of baroque splendor, the proceedings within a travesty of justice. Don Raffaele winks at the lawyer. Even Pasqualino seems to tolerate the knowledge that all of his sisters are now whores; they are working, after all, to pay for his defense. The camera pulls away from the jury; Pasqualino is declared totally insane and taken away in chains. So precise is the editing, the train taking him to the prison asylum seems an extension of the courtroom.

He sits in the waiting room at the train station in Averso with a socialist (Roberto Herlitzka), a political victim of the Fascists. He has been sentenced to serve twenty-eight and a half years, Pasqualino thirteen. The Fascist order of priorities is numerically clear: Political disagreement is twice as offensive as murder. Another spokesman for the director, the socialist praises creative disorder: "I bless the days of riots and strikes. They were symptoms of a curable disease." Pasqualino prefers as usual to praise the endurance of a more tangible reality—his own life preserved. "Il Duce's court allowed my insanity plea," he says of himself, then simplistically of his country, "Mussolini gave us an empire; he made other countries respect us." Ill at ease, even fearful, of the socialist's sentiments, Pasqualino tries to dominate the conversation. "I take things as they come," he speaks tellingly once again of himself, then of that city of "brotherhood" we have come to know through him, "Naples is a place of imagination."

Currying petty favor, Pasqualino gains a certain freedom in the asylum as an orderly. He is obviously saner—in a way—than most of its regular inmates. Checking a bedpan, he admonishes a patient: "To pee is to live; the more you pee the more you live." The instruction, a parody of medical care, is regrettably consistent with his biological fixation. Allowed to clean the women's ward, he shifts attention to his member's other function. Instruction yields to baser instinct. Starved for sex, he raises the gown of a woman strapped to a bed, inspecting his prize before attacking it. At the precise moment when he seems to have coaxed a passionate response, the woman bites him and screams. In rapid succession, the film cuts to the phases of Pasqualino's punishment. He is sprayed with a fire hose, put in a straightjacket, and given shock treatment. Unexpectedly, Pasqualino is spared his full fate. An elderly woman doctor (Doriglia Palmi) promises him freedom. (Is it always the maternal figure who condones the erring child in us?) "I want to live," he repeats. "I'll do anything to live." "They need men for the war," she responds clinically. "We'll get you out. This place is for sick people." And she is utterly serious in saying it. The moment is precise for an ironic cut, with voice-over, to the "sanity" of the concentration camp, and the beginning of the climactic final sequence of the film.

Pasqualino remains at attention in the center of the hall. He commences his last campaign (for mere life) by opening his mouth to sing. Though initially weak and dreadfully off-key, the strains of his love song eventually reach the second-story office of the commandant. She opens a small window, gazing down at her serenader with as much disbelief as her cold, dispassionate face can show. Summoned to his ultimate confrontation, Pasqualino is shoved onto the floor at the commandant's feet. "You shit macaroni!" she says with utter scorn. "I love you" is Pasqualino's dumb, but consistent response. "You hope your love will get you food," the commandant spits back. In his determination to live he has become a parody of Gospel perseverance. He will "prey" till he gets what he wants. There is yet another parody of the Gospels, central to the meaning of the film, that becomes transparent in this concluding sequence. Molly Haskell, evidently the first to point it out, seems curiously enough to think it not worth making. One can only wonder why. She calls it "a message, writ loud though rather late, to clear up the chronic confusion and give the audience something to take home."[12] It is certainly not "writ late"; and if it is "writ loud," it is not because it is expressed in so many words, but rather because it is the meaning that gradually emerges with appalling urgency from the very structure of the film itself. It is the negative warning of the paradox integral to Jesus' teaching: "Whoever seeks to save his life will lose it" (*The New English Bible,* Luke 17:33).

Pasqualino pursues his tired theme: "I don't think you're the way you seem to be." It is her sense of duty that makes her the way she is; she too is a victim, he claims. The commandant yields, but her manner suggests she will use him sexually and let him call it seduction. Her warning is stern: "Make love to me, then I'll kill you with my own hands." Undressing in layers, releasing mounds of flesh, then sitting, she is indeed a sight designed to test desire. A portrait of Hitler glares disapprovingly from the wall behind her. In that setting, the whip between her thighs is a firmer instrument than Pasqualino is able to produce. Wertmüller directs the foreplay with a master's eye for burlesque; the humor, though grotesque, is a relief. Pasqualino scales the mountain from one of the easier slopes, kissing rapidly up her arm from hand to shoulder, then biting quickly but firmly into a mammoth breast; he is like a mouse on a mountain of cheese, or in Pauline Kael's phrase, "like a fly settling on Mount Rushmore."[13] The perch is precarious, however; he slips headfirst into the valley of her thighs, his feet fanning the air.

Pasqualino is too weak to perform. "Eat, Naples!" she taunts, spotting a plate of food, as if for a dog, dead center to a swastika on the floor, with the added warning that he will die immediately if eating does not cure his impotence. On a sofa now for his second and last try, Pasqualino struggles like one who realizes that the problem is more psychological than pysiological. He closes his eyes and summons from memory images of Fifi, his first love. The commandant perceives his trick, and even though she pries open his eyes, he grunts and squirms his way to limited success, despite her icy refusal ever to respond. "Your thirst for life disgusts me," she says. "In Paris, a Greek made love to a goose. He did this to eat, to live. And you . . . you . . . you subhuman Mediterranean larva. You can have an erection and so you can survive . . . you subhuman worm with no ideals or ideas. And our dreams of a master race . . . unattainable."

But dreams of a master race and mere existence as a subhuman worm are only extremes superficially; in the physical coupling, of commandant and prisoner, we understand their fundamental similarity. Whatever the commandant has done Pasqualino can do too, even though till now it was only in a minor key. She appoints him *Kapo* of his stalag and instructs him to select six men for slaughter. On the floor against a wall of the commandant's office, Bronzino's "Venus, Cupid, Folly, and Time" stands, ironic commentary on her order. The painting shows Venus seducing Cupid, her son, so that he in turn, out of love, will destroy Psyche. The commandant has seduced Pasqualino and now she will force him to kill at her bidding. However, she is neither destroying his soul nor asking him to do it; her command is designed, in vain, to make him realize he has already destroyed it, to force him to acknowledge his own duplicity.

Pasqualino frantically searches the list of inmates, thinking that the impersonal method of choosing numbers at random will somehow diminish his crime. Pedro volunteers himself; Pasqualino refuses. The prisoners are assembled with haste in the vast hall; the commandant confidently awaits the execution of her order, the slow, almost orbital movement of her head and the unrelenting, penetrating stare of her eyes reminding us of the frozen limits of Dante's damned in the pit of Cocytus. Pasqualino calls out the numbers of the doomed. A tear forms on Pedro's cheek, a single sufficient word of protest on his lips. "Enough," he shouts, as he breaks ranks and runs for the latrines; he will die in shit rather than live in hell, he explains. Perhaps unnecessarily. The act is symbolic enough; and though its manner and articulation are crude, there is nothing whatever humorous about it. The S.S. guards riddle his submerged body with bullets. Pedro, ineffectual as an anarchist, chooses a mode of death that is superior in his mind to the slavery imposed by the men he had tried to assassinate. Though his cause, in Wertmüller's world, is doomed to failure, Pedro is still a man.

But what are we to make of Francesco? He prefers simply to die. "I'm tired of living in terror," he announces, as he falls to his knees at Pasqualino's feet. "You're a friend, shoot me," he begs. The terror of life there gnaws at his very guts. If Pasqualino refuses, he will soil his pants. In spite of his pathetic condition, perhaps Francesco too has a cause, but it is not the typical cause in Wertmüller's films. Francesco offers his life voluntarily for the sake of his friend; he and Pasqualino had after all been drawn together by something akin to friendship from the moment they deserted the army. In effect, his free offer of self would diminish the weight of Pasqualino's guilt. If Wertmüller wants us to believe that Francesco's sacrifice is unnecessary—the six Pasqualino had to choose for slaughter die anyway—she would never have made his dying the climactic moment of ritual it actually is.

Pasqualino hesitates—with reason. It seems improbable that he realizes the full irony of Francesco's sacrifice, that he offers his life for the liberation of Pasqualino's spirit; for in asking him to kill someone he knows, Francesco equivalently forces the issue of duplicity. Pasqualino can no longer bury his guilt in anonymity. Rather, Pasqualino balks at the thought (can we call it *mere*?) of killing a friend for whatever reason. His hesitation—for whatever reason—has little immediate effect; he is ordered to kill Francesco. The prisoners, filling the hall in orderly rank upon rank, kneel—inexplicably—as if on cue. It is indeed a sacred moment. All movement is frozen; there is utter silence. Pasqualino stands above the kneeling Francesco; a stationary camera watches Pasqualino's slow, painful elevation of the pistol trace an arc from his leg where it points harmlessly at the floor to its angle of lethal entry into Francesco's head. After what seems like an eternity, the shot is fired; Francesco slumps; dogs bark, straining at leash's end; the chosen six are summarily executed; and silence once again descends upon the hall, except for the strains of Iannaci's score, punctuated by a plaintive horn. A tracking shot slowly reviews the lines of kneeling prisoners, from the front; in one continuous movement—doubtlessly with the help of a crane—the camera pans up Pasqualino, still frozen where he killed Francesco, and moves out over the reverent bodies behind him into the haze enveloping the assembly.

Given the circumstances, perhaps Francesco is the closest

Wertmüller comes in her films to the *genuine* man. John Simon is certainly accurate when he says that "there is no absolute right"[14] in *Seven Beauties*. No image of man in this film, or in any of Wertmüller's for that matter, is *absolutely* right. On the other hand, Simon goes too far when he says that *all* "are right, or partly right." For Simon, "the simply decent Francesco" and "the complexly perceptive Pedro" are equally right.[15] "It is right to die defiantly in a vat of excrement; it is also right to survive by swallowing excrement," he claims.[16] To equate Pedro and Francesco is one thing, and easier to understand, if not accept; to claim the same of Pedro and Pasqualino is, however, the greatest treason: to praise Wertmüller (as Simon certainly does) for the wrong reason. To die in excrement is far closer to being right in Wertmüller's world than eating it. Whether it is better still to give one's life for one who swallows it is more precisely the question.

When the camera lifts up into the haze over the kneeling prisoners in the hall of the concentration camp, the film jump cuts to Naples and Pasqualino's return from the war. It is still the present time of the film, a concluding portion to its seventh and final sequence. The streets are alive with rejoicing. The war has ended; American sailors roam the streets, embracing at will the buxom Neapolitan women. Not just Pasqualino's sisters and mother, the whole city, it seems, has become a brothel for the conquering heroes—even the innocent young girl Pasqualino had earlier offered the protection of his manhood. Pauline Kael speaks of the "goofy, ebullient mood" with which Wertmüller presents the world as "a teeming bordello."[17] Bruno Bettelheim complains that "the implied moral is that those who overcome Fascism—in this case, the Americans—degrade even good human beings like this girl as effectively as the S.S. degraded prisoners in the camps."[18] One need not, with the film's sterner critics, exaggerate the meaning of this concluding impression. There is of course an element of sad realism in the picture she portrays. Yet this is, after all, the story of Pasqualino whose path to disintegration began when he "killed for a woman" to save face. What further commentary on his family's honor do we need? or on his city's honor, nurtured by the Brotherhood?

Obviously, whoever is uneasy with the film's implication of universal sin in its parting view of Naples must reject the Psalmist's suggestion that even the just man falls seven times daily.

Piercing the excitement of the street scene is Concettina's jubilant announcement to her mother: "Pasqualino's back!" His sisters rush to meet him; they are actually rushing toward the camera. What is so extraordinary about this brief final scene is the delay in Pasqualino's appearance. The camera, behind Pasqualino's mother, erupts into the place his family now calls home. No longer a curtained-off section in a mattress factory, their quarters reveal another sort of poverty. Everywhere are the cheap, gaudy touches of the prostitute. Pasqualino is still not visible; we see with his eyes a sickening montage of meretricious innocence. The focus of the camera passes quickly from a vulgar painting of Jesus in the foreground to a portrait of Pasqualino on the wall; there are the usual dolls on the neatly made beds. Pasqualino's mother holds out a new coat for her yet invisible son; in its thrust toward the camera, we know that we are being asked to understand the emptiness of return without renewal.

Then Pasqualino's young girl friend bursts through the doorway, happy but ashamed. As she rushes to greet him, we see him for the first time. He knows of course that her days of parrot and song are gone. "Even you've become a whore?" he asks without need of answer. "Quit," he proposes, "we'll get married and have kids. I want lots of kids . . . twenty-five . . . thirty. Soon they'll be killing one another for an apple. We've got to defend ourselves . . . there's got to be lots of us!" Pasqualino, ever estranged from the world of ideas and ideals, blends Pedro's view of the future with a contradictory Fascist program of procreation, one clear cause of the struggle for food. He has understood nothing of Pedro's "new man."

His mother interrupts. "Have a good look at yourself," she urges, "you're alive!" Once again, as it should, the camera dictates meaning. We see Pasqualino's face cut down the middle by the frame between two sections of a triptych mirror. There is at first neither Pasqualino nor his full reflection, only a split image shouting duplicity. Then we see his face, undivided, as his mother and the young girl move into the multiple mirror's view. To his mother's "Pasqualino, you're alive!" he can say merely, "Yes, I'm alive." There is little doubt that now Pasqualino knows, in his guts, the limits of his life. He is merely living; he can claim no more. The reflection of his sad, defeated face is frozen, as the girl's song is heard once again. It is not even the frozen reflection of a man, only the reflection of a man's shell—the macho without a cause.

Pasqualino (Giancarlo Giannini) and his sister Concettina (Elena Fiore) in *Seven Beauties*.

Conclusion
An Image of the Future

The longest and most developed, if not most important, essay on Lina Wertmüller to have as yet appeared in America is undoubtedly Bruno Bettelheim's "Surviving."[1] *Seven Beauties,* which it analyzes in detail, is generally considered to be the best of Wertmüller's films to date and is clearly a work to be reckoned with. Bettelheim's critique in its thoroughness raises issues that are central to Wertmüller's art, to her development as a director and screenwriter. Discussion of it is crucial, we feel, to an understanding of her achievement, particularly of the parabolic nature of her films.

Bettelheim, eminent psychologist and himself a survivor of the Holocaust, takes strong exception to what he considers the dangers both of Wertmüller's film and of Terrence Des Pres' recent work on the Nazi and Stalinist concentration camps, *The Survivor.* By coincidence, Terrence Des Pres did a shorter piece on *Seven Beauties* at about the same time.[2] Neither Bettelheim nor Des Pres seems aware of the other's comment on the film (Des Pres' point of departure is an article of Jerzy Kosinski's), yet the essays are decidedly complementary. It is certainly not our competence or domain here to judge Des Pres' work *The Survivor,* although we certainly find Bettelheim's position on survivorship, like Viktor Frankl's in *Man's Search for Meaning,* more appealing and reasonable philosophically and psychologically. Yet, regardless of what stand one may take on the subject of survivorship, itself or on Des Pres' book, there can be little doubt that Des Pres comes closer to understanding *Seven Beauties* than Bettelheim does. And the precise reason is this: *Seven Beauties* is not a treatise on survivorship, it is a film; hence it must be judged by artistic standards, not simply philosophical ones. This is not the same thing as saying that it need not correspond somehow with the reality we perceive. It is to say that we cannot expect a film to present all of reality or, more precisely, reality exactly as we perceive it. Film, like all art, creates its own world, and it is the total world of the film that must be judged for coherence, consistency, awareness of complexity, and imaginative integration. Correspondence with experience, which is also integral to aesthetic judgment, is not a simple comparison of the director's world with the critic's experience. The viewer must compare the work's total world with his own total experience; and the judgment of correspondence, in the words of Rene Wellek and Austin Warren, "registers itself in aesthetic terms of vividness, intensity, patterned contrast."[3]

Bettelheim seems concerned not so much with the acclaim the film received from critics and audiences alike, but rather with the way "it seems to shape their views about matters they had been little familiar with before, including the all-important issue of survivorship."[4] The positive response *Seven Beauties* has received suggests to Bettelheim that "one generation after the Nuremberg trials any justification of survivorship under Fascism seems to have become acceptable."[5] The film's view of survivorship that he considers so abhorrent is the same point, he claims, that Des Pres makes in his book. "According to them," Bettelheim writes, "the main lesson of survivorship is: all that matters, the only thing that is really important, is life in its crudest, merely biological form."[6] "To embrace life without reserve," Des Pres' understanding of the true lesson learned from survivorship, means living "beyond the compulsions of culture" and "by the body's crude claims."[7] "Wertmüller's film," Bettelheim adds, "gives these principles visible form and symbolic expression."[8]

Bettelheim's conclusion about the film is defective on two counts: He misunderstands art's distance from reality and makes excessive demands of the artist. The latter is never more clearly expressed than when he says without theoretical justification: "If a presentation of what is involved in survival is to have any meaning, it cannot restrict itself to stating simply that unless one remains alive one does not survive. It must tell what

Conclusion: An Image of the Future

else is needed: what one must be, do, feel; what attitudes, what conditions are required for achieving survival under concentration-camp conditions."[9] To begin with Bettelheim's "what else," two responses come quickly to mind. The first is that one cannot expect "story" to say everything, to do, for example, what the expository essay, more specifically philosophical argumentation, is designed to achieve. Bettelheim confuses genres. Secondly, and more obviously, he is building from a false premise, a misinterpretation of the film.

Bettelheim's aesthetic problem stems from his inability to see the whole for the parts. He is able at one moment with utter clarity to see that "the film is true to the realities of the concentration camp in a certain way" when it shows, through the consistency of Pasqualino's behavior before and during the war, that "prisoners did not suddenly begin to behave in the camps altogether differently from the way they had behaved in freedom."[10] And again, when he concedes that Pedro's hope for "a new man . . . who can rediscover harmony within himself" contains "the true lesson of the concentration camp," Bettelheim is accurate and precise: "From having not enough space to lie down at night, from living in starvation, the survivor ought to have learned that even under such conditions, or particularly under such conditions, one can discover a life of harmony which permits one to make do, to get along with others and to live in harmony also with oneself."[11] But because he is convinced that the film is about survivorship (and not about the universal implications of *this* particular mode of survival), he consistently fails in assessing the harmony of its parts.

Wertmüller does not equate survival with remaining alive. The film avoids any such statement. It is content rather to raise a question and, at best, imply its answer, since the way of art is invariably indirect. The question that *Seven Beauties* asks is whether merely being alive can be considered survival at all. The answer implied in the parallel structure of the film and in the characterization of Pasqualino is this: Merely being alive is the basest sort of human survival; in fact, it can scarcely be called human at all. Pasqualino "Seven Beauties" is a *mere macho*, a worm and no man.

Bettelheim's actual problem, infinitely more understandable considering his personal experience, is that he cannot forget the horror of his own imprisonment. This human problem, which nevertheless effectively blocks his appreciation of the film, stems from his conviction that there was and is nothing funny at all about concentration camps and that to laugh at all is to deny the horror of the Holocaust. But there is laughter and laughter, and the kind Wertmüller elicits is designed to preserve the reality of the very horror Bettelheim is afraid we will forget.

More attention to the structure of the film and the centrality of Pasqualino as a certain type of man—the macho without a cause—makes it abundantly clear that the concentration camp episode is necessary to demonstrate the full horror of this man. Appearances aside, the worm without ideals or ideas is no better than the dreamers of a master race. Genocide is killing for *dignità* writ large. Masters of the grostesque, and Wertmüller certainly is one, deal in such bold strokes. *Seven Beauties* is not about the limits of survivorship; it is a parable about the potential for catastrophe when even the reasonable concepts of honor and dignity are reduced to an absurdity.

Des Pres, whose view of the world and of survivorship does seem regrettably minimal, works toward an understanding of the film in the categories of art. He takes Jerzy Kosinski's rejection of *Seven Beauties* as "a cartoon trying to be a tragedy" and converts it into praise for all of Wertmüller's films. "Her films are just that," he suggests, "part cartoon, part tragedy, life's sorrow smeared in farce. This is an art faithful to life as we live it, half in joke and half in deadly earnest."[12] Des Pres feels that the greatest danger of art is its very capacity to order chaos, to convert life's terror and the possibility of disaster into the consolation of metaphor. "Taming the world through aesthetic mediation," he claims, "becomes a kind of moral betrayal because it promotes detachment and false hope."[13] It need not do the latter, that is, promote *false* hope, yet one must admit that the potential has always been there. Such a betrayal, we feel, results either from poor art or from the misinterpretation of great art.

Wertmüller's greatness, for Des Pres, lies precisely in her

Conclusion: An Image of the Future 73

capacity as an artist to block detachment by finding the means within art to subvert our tendency to facile hope. His description of her method could stand as an aesthetics of the parable. That method, he says, is "to present hard truths wrapped in laughter, to weave fact and parody of fact into a single striking whole, to give us rough slabs of reality stewing in their own exaggeration."[14] Our first response, writes Des Pres, to the comic presentation even of hard truths is laughter, a laughter at once liberating and implicating. We laugh at ourselves and our foibles, yet our very laughter implicates us in the deformity we witness. Parody, the second stage of her artistic method, and the inevitable effect of the parallel structure of her richer films, is designed to prevent us from escaping life's harsh problems. Her art succeeds, Des Pres concludes, "by allowing its content to flounder back and forth between facts savagely, lucidly intense and facts grotesquely exaggerated. And always it is the connection which counts—the connection between truths universally urgent through their political ramifications, and truths at the same time the stuff of life itself, slapstick and confused, at moments supremely funny but always, in the end, filled with absurdity and pain."[15] Once one has sold out, as Pasqualino obviously does, one's life becomes a perfect parody of itself, "to be acted out in an agony of loathing and loss."[16]

If Crossan is correct then in stating that *parable* subverts the world that *myth* establishes, and we are convinced that he is, Lina Wertmüller's films have functioned rather consistently—and intelligently—in a parabolic fashion toward the mythic claims and chauvinist bravado of Italian manhood, that curious marriage of sex and politics, more specifically of sexism and the ideological extremes of fascism-anarchy. Myths invariably project ideals as resolutions of tensions inherent in a situation, and popular Italian culture, perhaps more facilely than others, has certainly done that in terms of family honor and masculine dignity. Yet when projected ideals are thought to be realized *absolutes,* as has happened to *onore* and *dignità* particularly in southern Italy and Sicily, myth has begun to disintegrate and become the suitable target of parable. What Benito Mussolini demonstrated tragically for the twentieth century—"the limitations of showmanship," in Barzini's phrase[17]—the films of Lina Wertmüller re-present as visual parable and preserve aesthetically as lasting challenge to complacence. The very objection that some have raised about Wertmüller's pandering to Giancarlo Giannini's eyes, as if to suggest that she finally adores what she presents for scorn, becomes a touchstone of her art. That face, those eyes linger; indeed, they are unforgettable. What lingers is not directorial connivance but true artistic distance. To remember the face is to understand the pathetic limits of showmanship—to be disturbed once again. Ugo Ojetti's reflection on Mussolini comes to mind: "I cannot help thinking when I see him, how much his face must ache at night when he retires."[18] Barzini characterizes Mussolini's posture as "a heroic mixture of the Renaissance *condottiere,* the cold Machiavellian thinker, Lenin-like leader of a revolutionary minority, steely-minded dictator, humanitarian despot, Casanova lover, and Nietzchean superman."[19] None of Lina Wertmüller's machos, even those with a cause, approximates this stature. Yet she will not let us forget the potential is there, paradoxically, in her macho without a cause. Little wonder that *Love and Anarchy* and *Seven Beauties* begin with montages of Il Duce.

As Crossan analyzes myth and parable, and the stages between, it is clear that they are the extremes of story as a cycle. And although he does not directly explore this connection, it seems to us that the reaches of parable touch the reemergence of myth. At this stage in the development of her art, it is clear that Wertmüller has not resolved the tensions in the world of her work. She continues to disturb rather than console; in fact, with *Seven Beauties* highest art and deepest disturbance coincide. Yet she has Pedro, before his ritual suicide, sow the seeds of resolution. And the vision, though incomplete, is indeed consoling, at least the beginning of consolation, as myth is supposed to be. "I believe in man," Pedro announces, "but in a new man that must be born, a civilized man, . . . a new man who can rediscover harmony within himself. . . . That's the only hope . . . man in disorder." With the reemergence of myth's resolving images, we experience the taste of genuine hope that comes from

Conclusion: An Image of the Future 75

contact with the transcendent future of man. The acknowledged possibility of liberation and reconciliation is the basic goal of all religion, the very substance of man's belief in God.

"When I speak of man in disorder," Wertmüller says in the interview that ends this book, "I am talking about a man who even though he now and then makes mistakes is nevertheless growing in harmony with himself and the world." The *dis*order Wertmüller envisions as the hope of man is, we feel, better rendered as *dys*order. The Greek *dys* says less than the Latin *dis;* the former suggests "ill" or "poor" order; the latter, a privative, means "no" order at all. Anarchy is no resolution to human tensions; neither is total control (the Nazis had that!). The tolerance of something less than order, the pursuit of something more than chaos, *is*. These are the limits of solution.[20]

Wertmüller prizes our freedom to grow, to rediscover the harmony within. "Only when this condition of growth exists for men, for every single human being," she says in the interview, "can there be a possibility for that harmony which we seek in the place of order."[21] Between the disorder of anarchy and the order of fascism lies the acceptance of imperfection in the path to harmony—"man in dysorder."

Interview with Lina Wertmüller

The interview took place on October 25, 1976, at Lina Wertmüller's apartment in Rome. It began in English but then slipped very quickly into Italian. I was indispensably assisted in my comprehension of Italian by John Navone, S.J., a professor of the Gregorian University in Rome, who is the author of several books and articles on religion and culture.

—*Ernest Ferlita, S.J.*

E.F. I was sorry to hear that your film on Caligula would not be made, because I became very interested when you said in an interview with John Simon that it would be about "the great trap that is God." Would you be willing to say more about that idea?
WERTMÜLLER. You are turning the knife in my wound.
E.F. I realize that must have been a great disappointment.
WERTMÜLLER. I like very much the idea of my Caligula. I've been trying to get it done for ten years! When Guccione, the producer of [Gore Vidal's] Caligula, came to me, I told him I didn't see how I could do it. For two years we went on about it. Finally, I had to tell him it was impossible. I know Gore Vidal is a good writer, but I had my own ideas.[1] If you wait, I think you will see my Caligula.
E.F. I surely hope so.

WERTMÜLLER. It is necessary to be patient. I love my idea about this man Caligula. The historical Caligula was a very young man, very strange, very centralized. His situation was so special it is difficult for us to understand. *(Here she switches to Italian.)* He became emperor probably as the result of a series of crimes, which were nevertheless quite in accord with the times. They would be evaluated in a way very different from the way we'd evaluate them today. Certainly he achieved absolute power. The power of the Roman emperor—that is not easy for us to grasp. It would be as if he were the ruler of America *and* Russia and every other power—all summed up in one man. The greatest known power in the world. Then, at the moment of his ascendancy, he was struck down by a cerebral fever. I am speaking now of his true life story. He went into a spiral of madness. It's his madness that is interesting. If we think of the great tyrants, like Hitler, for example—Hitler tended to absolute power. He was convinced he was working for the people. He never suspected he was a monster. That's the irony. All the documents on Caligula are fascinating. Caligula thought that he was God, and he imagined he was always being betrayed by men. Therefore, he put himself in a very particular position vis-à-vis humanity. For rather base reasons he needed money: to put on his big spectaculars and to run his armies. And so he was always thinking of traps for men to fall into, inspired by the aristocratic concept of the Roman citizen. The Roman citizen had a great tradition of justice, and Caligula used it to set his traps. We find something like this in the behavior of the Nazis toward the Jews. For example, in Poland, they would ask the rabbis for the names of thirty men to save three hundred. Usually the rabbis were so desperate they would rather die themselves than make this decision. But sometimes they gave them the names, and the Nazis would give great publicity to what they did in order to discredit them (as well as the concept of the spiritual father) in the eyes of the Jews. Now this is similar to what Caligula did. It's a use that power often makes in its administration of justice when it wants to accomplish something unjust, namely, the besmirching of the very concept of justice as represented by certain men. The fathers of the Roman senate were symbols of justice. Caligula spent his life trying to show that they were men unworthy of the people's esteem. He would lay traps for them, get them into compromising situations, make them do abominable things, and in that way discredit them before the people. He did it to get money but mainly to dissociate himself from the concept of the Roman citizen, to put himself above it, to transcend its responsibilities and obligations, in order to exalt himself into the position of a god. In effect, he pushed everything toward corruption and then denounced the perpetrators of it. It is a very interesting mechanism, a mechanism that has operated throughout the history of man, with respect to power.

E.F. And this grasping for power is "the great trap that is God"?

WERTMÜLLER. Very often power outdoes itself in this way. Another variation of it is what happens in the Soviet Union. Russia is a country where people do not count for much. They have very little news there. For ages the same idea has operated in the Church—through the "dark" ages! *(Laughter)* But now the Church has other problems.

E.F. This idea is linked to another one of yours, is it not, to your concept of "man in disorder"?

WERTMÜLLER. Yes. I think we are living in very interesting but dangerous times. When I speak of man in disorder, I realize I am using a dangerous phrase. Because disorder is more fascinating than order. And that is terrifying. We see all around us mortal signs of disorder. But there is also a terrifying moment in the concept of order. I believe very profoundly in the concept of the growth of man. Only when this condition of growth exists for man, for every single human being, can there be any possibility for that harmony which we seek in the place of order. Order is understood here as something imposed from above, and therefore it has all the risks of concepts imposed from above, concepts or structures imposed from above. Harmony is certainly utopian. But when a man has achieved awareness, he can hope for utopia. The ways in which man has gone in pursuit of harmony throughout his history are many, the first of these being religion, in its original inspiration. All religions, in a certain sense, are the same with respect to the concept of man, i.e., of the man who achieves harmony with all that surrounds him, with life, with others, with himself. When I speak of man in disorder, I am talking about a man who even though he now and then makes mistakes is nevertheless growing in harmony with himself and the world. In the original script of *Seven Beauties* that little phrase "man in disorder" was part of a monologue written for the anarchist that went on for fifty pages. Cited in those pages was that stupendous scene by Thomas Mann from his book *The Magic Mountain* in which he recounts the conversation between the Jesuit and the socialist.[2] He presents the concept of faith and of rationalism in a new relationship. He presents them in a way remarkable for his time. What we are given is the concept of the new man, of harmonious man, and he shows how this man can be born through faith, through intelligence, through humanism, through the maturation of society. The whole presentation may strike one as theoretical, but it is so relevant for a world that seems to be rushing headlong towards destruction, lacking all good sense and reason. Yes, man seems to be rushing towards destruction; and yet there are all those other resources, whether religion or reason or culture, that are positive forces for man's harmony.

J.N. When you talk about disorder or anarchy, you tend to oppose those things that stifle man's growth. You bring to mind what St. Paul said about the tension between law and spirit. Your notion of anarchy seems to correspond to his notion of spirit. And your notion of imposed structures to a very formalistic application of law. Because what counts for both you and St. Paul is the growth and development of the human spirit.

WERTMÜLLER. Definitely.

J.N. I've always felt that Italy operates on the jazz principle, on a principle of perpetual improvisation. The laws and structures in Italy are something like a beanpole. Your anarchy and Paul's spirit are the vine that grows around the pole.

WERTMÜLLER. Just so. An imposed order is stifling. We have some terrible proofs of this. I've always been a person of the left, but the history of art in the Soviet Union has been dreadful. There were many great artists and intellectuals who helped bring about the revolution, but then they were alienated be-

cause insofar as they were individuals who could quarrel with it they were considered harmful. An imposed order is dangerous in every area of life, even in the Church, when we remember how it retarded important historical developments. One must try to understand at what historical moment a certain form of order came to be.
J.N. In fact, for Jesus himself, it was from organized religion that his principal enemies came.
WERTMÜLLER. Certainly.
E.F. Jesus, then, was "man in disorder" relative to the pharisaical order of the day.
WERTMÜLLER. Exactly. Jesus always tried to show in extraordinary ways what man was all about. Like St. Francis of Assisi. That's why Dostoevsky is so remarkable in his portrayal of the Grand Inquisitor. This was the very problem he was dealing with—the problem of political order and power. It's a very great human theme. One of the greatest. Always under discussion. But beyond words there is always the truth that is difficult. In our age we must make ourselves go beyond them, because we are faced with a series of unarrestable social misdeeds, such as overpopulation. Already we number four billion people. What's going to happen in fifteen or twenty years? And then there's science, with its perilous research projects—the mysterious bomb whose consequences it does not know. And this fact has its impact on human nature. I have my days of pessimism when I just fear we are not going to make it.
E.F. In *Seven Beauties* Pasqualino's salvation is "to survive."
WERTMÜLLER. But of course that kind of salvation is a death.
E.F. Where does the vision come for a man like this?
WERTMÜLLER. It comes from the other character, from the anarchist, the one who says that man must achieve his harmony as quickly as possible. But it's not a vision so much as an intuition of the times. With respect, for instance, to massacre. In all those pages I cut out there was a link with all the great massacres of history—the massacre by the Spaniards of the Indians, of the Aztecs, the Incas; the massacre by the Inquisition; so many others. When we read the figures of these massacres, including that of the Jews—we get some idea of the

massacres that could occur under the pressure of overpopulation. All the scientific tests on the relationship of aggressivity to overpopulation are nightmarish. The man who has a certain harmony with his own space reacts very differently from the man in disharmony. In experiments with rats, aggressivity rises in proportion to overpopulation. Certainly this is a major problem, like the problem of pollution. Of very immediate concern.

E.F. There is still the question of woman as it relates to man's predicament, as you describe it. In *Love and Anarchy* love was represented by one woman, anarchy by another. In *The Seduction of Mimi* I have the impression that love and anarchy coexist in the character of Fiore. Do you see her as a kind of ideal that shows man what he should aim for?

WERTMÜLLER. I'm going to confess something to you. I don't make a distinction between man and woman in this sense. My characters are symbols for me of certain things having to do with human beings, quite independently of their sex. I don't believe in the distinction of the sexes. *(Laughing)* The Council of Trieste spent three centuries trying to establish that woman had a soul.[3] You can understand how they came to this conclusion, since the Roman matron had even more than a soul, she had tremendous power. Latium [the region of Rome] was a matriarchal society. However, I want to say that I reject every distinction between man and woman. This is so true that in my film *Swept Away* I have the woman representing industrial society and the man representing the third world. However, it could just as easily be the other way around because as often as not you find the woman playing the role of the third world. For example, the most obscure proletarian, when he comes home, gives vent to all the frustration and humiliation he has endured during the day by making his wife "the third world," by making her the butt of his rage. This presents a great problem for future societies regarding feminism. The day that man loses this woman upon whom he relies for so many services, he will become even more fragile than he is now. This imports a great change in the family structure. In this case, as in so many others, if you look with attention, the Church has given some

very important directions, because the monastic or conventual concept is a great one. I believe that only the creation of communities will enable man to survive this blasting of the atom that was the family. Once the atom or the molecule of the family is broken up, society loses a great element of its equilibrium. Especially if you don't put an end to overpopulation. It's indispensable to arrive at a concept of group, of commune. This has nothing to do with any silly sexual idea. Today we're bombarded with sex. I am obviously against any type of censorship. But the identification of pornography with liberty is something that I reject outright. I am constantly called upon to support causes that I *have* to support for conformity's sake. You cannot but support causes for total freedom of expression. *(Chuckling)* On the other hand, I have to admit that I am continually faced with the absurdity of identifying pornography with liberty. I have a great respect for human sensitivities and sentiments. And so I don't think there's any relationship between the concept of pornography and the fostering of authentic human development. Assuredly, pornography is more easily a loss than a gain, just as the concept of sin is a loss. But if we get rid of the concept of sin, everything seems to lose its fascination. This construction, which has been erected for so many centuries, is a delicate one. It has brought man to a sense of mystery, of fear, of vitality, of his own desires, of the possibility of sublimating them or of expressing them through his own body and intelligence. The breakdown, historical and therefore inexorable, of so many delicate equilibriums leaves man with all his values destroyed, bombarded, without putting in their place anything that conduces to his harmony. *(A pause)* You're a Jesuit, aren't you?
E.F. Yes, both of us.
WERTMÜLLER. You Jesuits have always been great workers in this field. Wonderful interpreters of the human soul. Great historians of the human spirit. St. Ignatius especially. A great genius. And all of your schools!
J.N. Do you know Father Arrupe, the general of the Jesuits?
WERTMÜLLER. I don't know him personally.
J.N. I think you would find him very similar in temperament to you. He has a profound rapport with the contemporary world and a genius for addressing it.

WERTMÜLLER. That is the way of the Jesuits. They are great experimenters. Do you know the drama called *The Sacred Experiment*? It's about the anarchical, socialist experiment that the Jesuits made in South America.
E.F. Oh, yes, in English it's called *The Strong Are Lonely*.
J.N. Yes, all about the reductions in Paraguay.
WERTMÜLLER. And the necessity of having to work out that very difficult equation between faith and knowledge.
J.N. The same improvisation was made by Father Ricci in China, adapting the faith to its culture.[4]
WERTMÜLLER. Exactly. It's in this way that a true salvation can come about for the Church. The Church has never in a thousand years been in such a perilous state as it is in today. What's needed is more than just having the priest turn around and say Mass in Italian. I mix with a lot of people of the south, with the poor, with women; I've talked to them a lot. And they're very opposed to all these changes in the liturgy. They wouldn't go as far as the French in their insubordination with regard to Vatican II, like Lefebvre, I mean. But it was an elitist decision rather than the kind of grassroots decision that the Church has always made in the past. The Church is wise. *(Laughing)* It has usually waited for fashions to pass before making crucial decisions. And this business of putting a cement altar in the middle of the church! *(Laughing)* It does violence to the beauty of the church; the churches just weren't built for that. I remember when I was a child listening to the women saying the Ave Maria, even though they didn't know the Latin. There were these sounds apparently devoid of meaning; what they conveyed was an overall meaning rather than the meaning of any particular word; the words *represented* prayer.
J.N. It was a kind of self-transcendence.
WERTMÜLLER. Yes, because in the subconscious there is a very profound sense of mystery. Mystery has always been the great support for all the comforts of religion. Even for fear. The comfort of fear must be as mysterious as fear itself. It can't be rationalized in a catechism. I had a conflict with the Church when I was young, a great conflict, which may sound rather silly if I try to explain how it came about in me. I was thirteen years old when I reflected on the first principles of the catechism. I

reasoned on this equation that was proposed to me: God is omniscient, omnipresent, omnipotent. Therefore he knows all, he wills all. Then he decided to create humanity, *the way it is*, with free will, knowing (because he is omniscient) all that would happen, with man placed within the confines of good and evil and with his great facility for slipping into evil. And so if at the end of all this you propose to me a heaven and a hell, I have to think that this omniscient God knows from the beginning that he will construct a series of eternal miseries. He has himself constructed the whole mechanism, and therefore he is bad![5] You laugh, but this is what brought about a revolution in me. I refuted every concept of faith, didn't I? This was no way to teach me catechism; you ought to tell me rather that God is a mystery. *(Laughing)* If you're going to teach me catechism, you shouldn't base it on premises I can so easily refute. I have no problem with free will, but I don't like the idea of free will opening the gates of hell. Even if one single human being goes to hell, God is bad. *(Laughing)* On this point I fought with everybody, with all the priests and all the nuns, and I broke my links with the Church.
E.F. I have a feeling that the Church betrays itself when it is too literal in conceptualizing its beliefs.
WERTMÜLLER. That's exactly what I was saying when I spoke of all those changes in the ritual. The ritual was full of mystery.
E.F. You need the image to preserve the mystery.
WERTMÜLLER. Definitely.
J.N. This has always been the strength of the great myths—the myths of Paradise, of Adam and Eve, of Moses, because the myths are not doctrine.
WERTMÜLLER. I agree.
J.N. Myths are always open, and you can reflect upon them for further insight into the mystery they attempt to convey. Once, when I was studying the Old Testament, a classmate of mine asked the professor: "Wouldn't it have been better if Von Ranke [a theologian] had written Genesis instead of that mythmaker? With Von Ranke we would have known right off what was true or false." The professor answered: "No. When you speak of mystery, myth is far more appropriate."
WERTMÜLLER. Bravo.

J.N. "You can't imprison mystery in a phrase."
WERTMÜLLER. The Jesuit in *The Magic Mountain* says the same thing. It's quite extraordinary because he comes to the conclusion that a great mystery, if it becomes the object of faith, thereby becomes the truth. Magnificent. You should reread this passage.[6]
E.F. Would you say that your films are attempts to construct new myths for modern man?
WERTMÜLLER. What I hope to express in my films is my great faith in the possibility of man becoming human. I have to set man up against society because I believe that the concept of the masses is a dangerous thing. It frightens me. The masses live according to the law of the anthill. I believe the greatest danger for man lies in this kind of anthill existence. Therefore the greatest defense for man, with all his intelligence, is to understand that *he* is society. Therefore, if I have children, I am one and all. I am one become five. It's my end, and everybody's end. There's no more harmony. When the Bible says, "Increase and multiply, as the grains of sand in the desert," you should interpret that ironically. If you increase and multiply like the grains of sand in the desert, you will *have* a desert. (Repeating the word with great emphasis.) *Un de-ser-TO! (Laughter)*
E.F. Now for a final question of fact. You mentioned Thomas Mann, Dostoevsky, the Bible. Were there any other intellectual influences in your life?
WERTMÜLLER. I really wouldn't know how to answer that because there were many and none. I believe that we are all the other. We are everything that has been: We are cellular which is more than being culturally united. Cellular. I am not a very learned person, but I am very much alive. I love people very much. I believe in life. I enjoy it. I believe in my work. I believe in action, and my way is not to create living beings but to create culture in life. I do whatever I can to contribute to harmony. If I were to say how many people were influences in my life—certainly there are many people I have loved, many who have enlightened me. I can speak of my most recent passion, *(repeating the phrase in English)* "my last love." "My last love" is Ceronetti. Do you know Ceronetti? *(She takes a book down from*

one of the shelves.) La carta è stanca [Paper Is Tired] by Guido Ceronetti. He is an intellectual, an Italian essayist, a young man of thirty-five living in Rome. I can read a little of him to show you something of his thought. Here's something he wrote at the end of 1975, a message for the New Year. Something stupendous. May I read you part of it?
E.F. & J.N. By all means.
WERTMÜLLER. *(Reading)* "If only people would understand that above all they need to get their breath again! They need a rest from history! A generous letting go, a pulling back, a slowing down, economic, demographic, industrial, scientific! Less industry, less money, fewer universities, fewer shows, fewer newspapers, less smoke! Silence. Truce. Little occupations. A few books. Not to have to go to the bathroom so badly. To die on time. Not to go around clawing in a sewer for a gigantic, imposed idea pulled up by black rats out of an intellectual language towards the clogged foundations to a dead end. . . . For an excess of civilization we are losing it."[7]

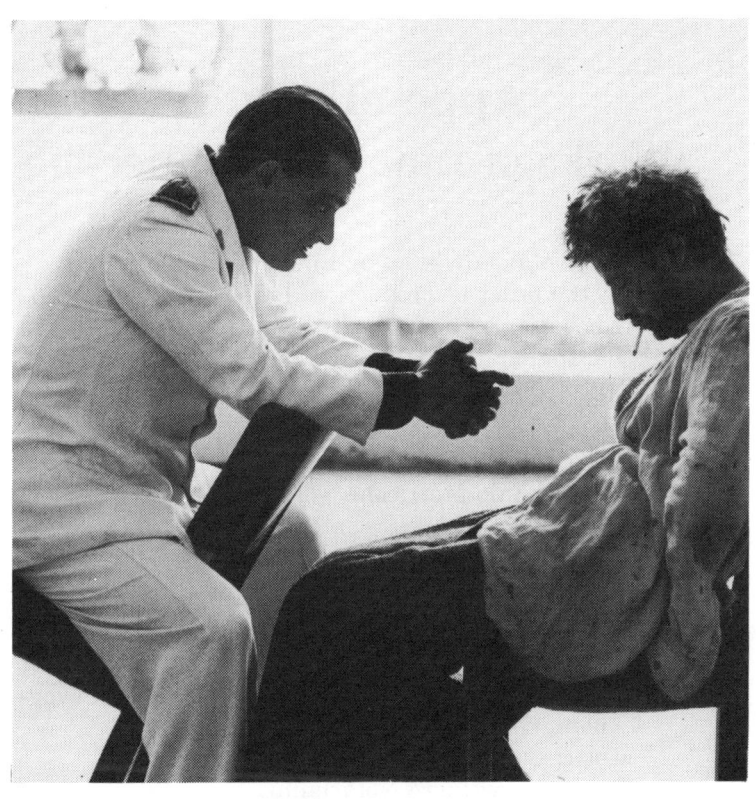

Spatoletti (Eros Pagni) and Tunin (Giancarlo Giannini) in *Love and Anarchy*.

Appendix A
Works of Lina Wertmüller

FILMS: Written and directed by Lina Wertmüller
(In the order of production and original release. A translation of the Italian title is given in parenthesis; the English title is given directly below.)

1963 *I Basilischi* (The Lizards)
Photography: Gianni di Venanzo
Editing: Ruggero Mastroianni
Music: Ennio Morricone

1965 *Questa volta parliamo di uomini* (This Time Let's Talk About Men)
Let's Talk About Men
Photography: Ennio Guarnieri
Editing: Ruggero Mastroianni
Art Direction: Paolo Tomassi, Ferdinando Giovagnoni, Giorgio Hermann
Music: Luis Enriquez Bacalov
Produced by: Piero Notarianni

1971 *Mimi metallurgico ferito nell'onore* (Mimi, Metalworker, Wounded in Honor)
The Seduction of Mimi
Photography: Dario di Palma
Editing: Franco Fraticelli
Art Direction: Enrico Job, Amedeo Fago
Music: Piero Piccioni
Produced by: Romano Cardarelli, Daniele Senatore

1972 *Film d'amore e d'anarchia, ovvero Stamattina alle 10 in via dei fiori nella nota casa di tolleranza* (Film of Love and Anarchy, *or* At 10 o'clock This Morning on the Via dei Fiori in a Well-Known Bordello)

Love and Anarchy
Photography: Giuseppe Rotunno
Editing: Franco Fraticelli
Art Direction: Enrico Job
Music: Carlo Savina
Songs: Nino Rota
Produced by: Romano Cardarelli

1973 *Tutto a posto e niente in ordine* (Everything's OK but Nothing Works)
All Screwed Up
Photography: Giuseppe Rotunno
Editing: Franco Fraticelli
Art Direction: Enrico Job
Music: Piero Piccioni
Produced by: Romano Cardarelli

1974 *Travolti da un insolito destino nell'azzuro mare d'agosto*
Swept Away by an Unusual Destiny in the Blue Sea of August
Photography: Ennio Guarnieri
Editing: Franco Fraticelli
Art Direction: Enrico Job
Music: Piero Piccioni
Produced by: Romano Cardarelli

1975 *Pasqualino Settebellezze* (Pasqualino Seven-Beauties)
Seven Beauties
Photography: Tonino delli Colli
Editing: Franco Fraticelli
Art Direction: Enrico Job
Music: Enzo Iannaci
Produced by: Lina Wertmüller, Giancarlo Giannini, Arrigo Colombo

TELEVISION MUSICALS

1966 *Rita la zanzara* (Rita the Mosquito)

Script: Lina Wertmüller, from a story by Sergio Bonotti
Direction: Lina Wertmüller (under the name "George Brown")
Photography: Dario di Palma
Editing: Franco Fraticelli
Art Direction: Fabrizio Frisardi
Music: Bruno Canfora
Produced by: Sergio Bonotti and Gilberto Carbone

1967 *Non stuzzicate la zanzara* (Don't Tease the Mosquito)
Script and Direction: Lina Wertmüller
Photography: Dario di Palma
Editing: Franco Fraticelli
Art Direction: Enrico Job, Fabrizio Frisardi
Music: Bruno Canfora
Produced by: Sergio Bonotti and Gilberto Carbone

COLLABORATOR ON FILM SCRIPTS FOR OTHER DIRECTORS

1969 *Les Chemins de Kathmandu/Katmandu*
1970 *Città violenta*
1970 *Quando le donne avevano la coda*
1972 *Quando le donne persero la coda* (story only)
1972 *Fratello sole sorella luna* (also story)
1973 *Cari Genitori*

ASSISTANT DIRECTOR

1963 8½

TELEVISION

1959 *Canzonissima* (Collaborator)
1961 *Piccolo Concerto* (Collaborator)
1965 *Il giornalino di Gian Burrasca* (Co-adaptor; director)
1966 *Studio Uno* (Drafter of text)

RADIO

1957   *Un Olimpo poco tranquillo* (co-author)
Adaptations of Chekhov
Collaboration on a number of musical variety shows

THEATRE

1968   *Due più due non fa più quattro*
1969   *La cucina* (adaptor & director of Wesker's *The Kitchen*)

Appendix B
Reviews of the Films

Let's Talk About Men

    Gilliatt, Penelope. "The Stronger Sex." *The New Yorker* 52 (August 16, 1976), 82, 85-86.

The Seduction of Mimi

    Biskind, Peter. "Lina Wertmüller: The Politics of Private Life." *Film Quarterly* 28:2 (Winter 1974-75), 10-16.

Love and Anarchy

    Biskind, Peter. "Lina Wertmüller: The Politics of Private Life." *Film Quarterly* 28:2 (Winter 1974-75), 10-16.
    Pechter, William S. "Watching Lina Wertmüller." *Commentary* 61 (January 1976), 75-77.

All Screwed Up

    Allen, Tom. "Announcing—Lina Wertmüller, Daredevil Aerialist." *America* 134 (February 7, 1976), 99-100.
    Callenbach, Ernest. "Everything Ready, Nothing Works." *Film Quarterly* 28:2 (Winter 1974-75), 59-60.
    Hatch, Robert. *Nation* 222 (January 31, 1976), 123-24.
    Kroll, Jack. "Wertmüller's Inferno." *Newsweek* 87 (January 26, 1976), 78-79.
    Wood, Michael. "All Mixed Up." *The New York Review of Books* (March 18, 1976), 5,8.

Swept Away

    Cocks, Jay. "Island Idyl." *Time* 106 (October 6, 1975), 65-66.
    Crist, Judith. *Saturday Review* 3 (November 1, 1975), 49.

Garson, Barbara. *Ms.* 4 (December 1975), 37-38.
Gilliatt, Penelope. "Vivid Doldrums." *The New Yorker* 51 (September 22, 1975), 94-95.
Haskell, Molly. "Swept Away on a Wave of Sexism." *The Village Voice* (September 29, 1975), back page, 114.
Hatch, Robert. *Nation* 221 (October 4, 1975), 318.
McCormick, Ruth. *Cineaste* (Spring 1976), 41.
Orth, Maureen. "Roman Candles." *Newsweek* 86 (October 6, 1975), 84.
Pechter, William S. "Watching Lina Wertmüller." *Commentary* 61 (January 1976), 75-77.
Porter, Carolyn, and Thomas, Paul. *Film Quarterly* 29:3 (Spring 1976), 49-53.
Wood, Michael. "All Mixed Up." *The New York Review of Books* (March 18, 1976), 4,8.

Seven Beauties

Allen, Tom. "Announcing—Lina Wertmüller, Daredevil Aerialist." *America* 134 (February 7, 1976), 99-100.
Canby, Vincent. "An Epic Film About Honor and Survival." *The New York Times,* Arts and Leisure (January 25, 1976), 1,15.
Cocks, Jay. "Charnel Knowledge." *Time* 107 (January 26, 1976), 76.
Crist, Judith. *Saturday Review* 3 (February 21, 1976), 49-50.
DiPiero, William S. "Wertmüller." *The American Poetry Review* 5:4 (July-August 1976), 45-47.
Hatch, Robert. *Nation* 222 (February 7, 1976), 155-56.
Kael, Pauline. "Seven Fatties." *The New Yorker* 51 (February 16, 1976), 104, 107-109.
Kosinski, Jerzy. "'Seven Beauties'—A Cartoon Trying to be a Tragedy." *The New York Times,* Arts and Leisure (March 7, 1976), 1,15.
Kroll, Jack. "Wertmüller's Inferno." *Newsweek* 87 (January 26, 1976), 78-79.
McMurtry, Larry. *"All the President's Men, Seven Beauties,* History, Innocence, Guilt, Redemption, and the Star System." *American Film* 1:9 (July-August 1976), 6-7, 78-79.

Pechter, William S. "Obsessions." *Commentary* 61 (May 1976), 72-76.

Simon, John. "Wertmüller's 'Seven Beauties'—Call It a Masterpiece." *New York* 9:5 (February 2, 1976), 24-31.

Westerbeck, Colin L., Jr. "Beauties and the Beast: *Seven Beauties/Taxi Driver.*" *Sight and Sound* 45:3 (Summer 1976), 134-39.

Wood, Michael. "All Mixed Up." *The New York Review of Books* (March 18, 1976), 5,8.

Appendix C
General Bibliography

Anon. "The Irresistible Force and the Immutable Object." *Time* 107 (February 16, 1976), 58-60.

Bettelheim, Bruno. "Surviving." *The New Yorker* 52:24 (August 2, 1976), 31-52.

Blumenfeld, Gina. "The (Next to) Last Word on Lina Wertmüller." *Cineaste* 7:2 (Spring 1976), 2-5, 50.

Des Pres, Terrence. "Bleak Comedies: Lina Wertmüller's Artful Method." *Harper's* 252 (June 1976), 26-28.

Garson, Barbara. "The Wertmüller Ethic." *Ms.* 4:11 (May 1976), 71-75, 128.

Gerard, Lillian. "The Ascendance of Lina Wertmüller." *American Film* 1:7 (May 1976), 20-27.

Haskell, Molly. "Lina Wertmüller Is a Radical Chick With an Eye for the Rooster." *The Village Voice* (January 26, 1976), 12-13.

Jacobs, Diane. "Lina Wertmüller: The Italian Aristophanes?" *Film Comment* 12:2 (March-April 1976), 48-50.

McIsaac, Paul, and Blumenfeld, Gina. "You Cannot Make the Revolution on Film: An Interview with Lina Wertmüller." *Cineaste* 7:2 (Spring 1976), 6-9.

Morini, Simone. "What Makes A Great Italian Actor? Ham." *The Village Voice* (February 2, 1976), back page, 79, 81.

Orth, Maureen. "Look This Way. Breathe. Brava!" *Newsweek* 87 (January 26, 1976), 79.

Quacinella, Lucy. "How Left is Lina?" *Cineaste* 7:3 (Fall 1976), 15-17.

Riley, Brooks. "Lina Wertmüller: The Sophists' Norman Lear?" *Film Comment* 12:2 (March-April 1976), 49, 51.

Stoop, Norma McLain. "Lina Wertmüller and Giancarlo Giannini: Cinematic Counterpoint." *After Dark* 8:12 (April 1976), 34-43.

Willis, Ellen. "Is Lina Wertmüller Just One of the Boys?" *Rolling Stone* (March 25, 1976), 31, 70, 72.

Zito, Tom. "Her Offspring: Films Born of Love, Anarchy and Economics." *The Washington Post,* Style (February 2, 1976), 1-2.

Notes

INTRODUCTION: MYTH AND PARABLE

1. Amos N. Wilder, "The Rhetoric of Ancient and Modern Apocalyptic," paper read before the American Academy of Religion, 1970, xeroxed, p. 4-5.
2. Charles B. Ketcham, *Federico Fellini: The Search for a New Mythology* (New York: Paulist Press, 1976), p. 6.
3. *Ibid.*, pp. 4-5.
4. John Dominic Crossan, *The Dark Interval: Towards a Theology of Story* (Niles, Illinois: Argus Communications, 1975), Ch. 2, *passim*.
5. Cf. Dan Otto Via, Jr., *The Parables: Their Literary and Existential Dimension* (Philadelphia: Fortress Press, 1967).
6. John Simon, "Wertmüller's 'Seven Beauties'—Call It a Masterpiece." *New York* 9:5 (February 2, 1976), 31.

PART ONE: THE ARTIST AND HER WORLD

1. From an interview for *Rai Radiotelevisione Italiana.*
2. Although most of the American writers who covered Wertmüller's promotional visit to the United States in 1976 gave her age as 47, Wertmüller herself wrote one of the authors that she was born in 1932. Brief reflection on the references she has made to her age elsewhere suggests now that the insistence was at best playful. In an interview with *Time,* she is quoted as saying she was born "somewhere between 1812 and 1928, I'll never say precisely"—a statement that makes 49 closer to the truth, as of 1977. "The Irresistible Force and the Immutable Object," *Time* 107 (February 16, 1976), 59.
3. *Rai Radiotelevisione Italiana.*
4. From the interview in this book, p. 84.
5. John Simon, "Portrait of the Artist as Workhorse," *New York* 9:5 (February 2, 1976), 30.
6. "The Irresistible Force and the Immutable Object," *Time* 107 (February 16, 1976), 59.
7. *Rai Radiotelevisione Italiana.*
8. Ennio Cavalli, *"Travolta da un insolito successo,"* **Paese Sera* (November 22, 1976), 4.
9. *Ibid.*
10. Lucy Quacinella, "How Left is Lina?" *Cineaste* 7:3 (Fall 1976), 16-17; Paul McIsaac and Gina Blumenfeld, "You Cannot Make the Revolution on Film: An Interview with Lina Wertmüller," *Cineaste* 7:2 (Spring 1976), 7; John Simon, "Wertmüller's 'Seven Beauties'—Call It a Masterpiece," *New York* 9:5 (February 2, 1976), 29.

11. Lillian Gerard, "The Ascendance of Lina Wertmüller," *American Film* 1:7 (May 1976), 25; Penelope Gilliatt, "The Stronger Sex," *The New Yorker* 52 (August 16, 1976), 85; Diane Jacobs, "Lina Wertmüller: The Italian Aristophanes?" *Film Comment* 12:2 (March-April 1976), 48, 50; Brooks Riley, "Lina Wertmüller: The Sophists' Norman Lear?" *Ibid.*, 51.

12. Quacinella, "How Left is Lina?" 5, 17.

13. Jacobs, "The Italian Aristophanes?" 48; Riley, "The Sophists' Norman Lear?" 51; Michael Wood, "All Mixed Up," *The New York Review of Books* (March 18, 1976), 5, 8; Pauline Kael, "Seven Fatties," *The New Yorker* 51 (February 16, 1976), 104, 109; Tom Allen, "Announcing—Lina Wertmüller, Daredevil Aerialist," *America* 134 (February 7, 1976), 99.

14. Simon, "Wertmüller's 'Seven Beauties,'" 24.

15. Vincent Canby, "An Epic Film About Honor and Survival," *The New York Times*, Arts and Leisure (January 25, 1976), 15; Wood, "All Mixed Up," 8; Molly Haskell, "Lina Wertmüller Is a Radical Chick With an Eye for the Rooster," *The Village Voice* (January 26, 1976), 13.

16. Simon, "Wertmüller's 'Seven Beauties,'" 26, 27.

17. Barbara Garson, "The Wertmüller Ethic," *Ms.* 4:11 (May 1976), 72.

18 See Eugene C. Kennedy, *The New Sexuality, Myths, Fables, and Hang-ups* (New York: Image Books, 1972), p. 15.

PART TWO: THE PARABLES OF LINA WERTMÜLLER

I. IMAGES OF WORLD

1. Luigi Barzini, *The Italians* (New York: Atheneum Publishers, 1964), p. 117.

2. A chronology of Wertmüller's films is given in Appendix A; it should be evident by now that chronology is never a principle of structure in this book. *All Screwed Up* (1974) is a middle film; *Seven Beauties* (1976), her latest to be released. As of this writing, Wertmüller is at work in Calabria on her eighth film, her first English-language film, tentatively titled *The End of the World in Our Usual Bed in a Night Full of Rain,* starring Giancarlo Giannini and Candice Bergen.

3. These parallels to Eisenstein's final film were brought to our attention by John Mosier of the Film Buffs Institute of Loyola University in New Orleans.

4. A simile used in a review of the film by John Stevens in the *Florida Flambeau* (May 14, 1976), 7.

II. IMAGES OF WOMAN

1. Ellen Willis, "Is Lina Wertmüller Just One of the Boys?" *Rolling Stone* (March 25, 1976), 31, 72; Molly Haskell, "Swept Away on a Wave of Sexism," *Village Voice* (September 29, 1975), 114.

2. John Simon, "Wertmüller's 'Seven Beauties'—Call it a Masterpiece," *New York* 9:5 (February 2, 1976), 29; Paul McIsaac and Gina Blumenfeld, "You Cannot Make the Revolution on Film," *Cineaste* 7:2 (Spring 1976), 8; "The Irresistible Force and the Immutable Object," *Time* (February 16, 1976), 58.

3. *Antepilulian,* a word coined in the fashion of *antebellum* and *antediluvian.*

The pill divides one age from another just as surely as any war or flood.
   4. Michael Wood, "All Mixed Up," *The New York Review of Books* (March 18, 1976), 5.
   5. One may wonder why Wertmüller does not have her implicate the Vatican. Perhaps because the context is not rich enough to support all the moral implications of the act. Legalized abortion is one of those unqualified demands on which Wertmüller is with the feminists "to the death." One could wish that she would approach the question from her anti-sexist principle: "The important thing is to be a human being."
   6. *Time,* 59.
   7. Wood, "All Mixed Up," 8.
   8. McIsaac and Blumenfeld, "You Cannot Make the Revolution on Film," 7.
   9. *Ibid.,* p. 8.
   10. *Ibid.*
   11. One would have to say that the later scenes of sexual surrender are nothing if not erotic, to a point where it could be argued that Wertmüller indulges herself beyond her avowed intentions. There is also one erotic scene in *The Seduction of Mimi:* the scene in which Fiore's understanding love gives Mimi back his potency, and the camera plays upon her face as she yields her virginity to him.
   12. *The Divine Milieu* (New York: Harper & Row, 1960), p. 74.
   13. Carolyn Porter and Paul Thomas, "Swept Away," *Film Quarterly* 29:3 (Spring 1976), 52.
   14. Luigi Barzini, *The Italians* (New York: Atheneum Publishers, 1964), p. 173.

III. IMAGES OF MAN

   1. It is the only one of Wertmüller's films that has not to date (Summer 1977) been publicly viewed in the United States.
   2. The film is marred technically by a poorly edited portion of the dinghy sequence at sea. The cut is from a long shot of a deep sunset, to a close shot of Gennarino struggling with the motor against a much brighter background, then back to the sunset, and again to Gennarino working in light. Although it is easy to understand how one would balk at discarding what is an extraordinarily beautiful sunset shot, the intercutting is altogether unnecessary and visually offensive.
   3. Peter Biskind, "Lina Wertmüller: The Politics of Private Life," *Film Quarterly* 28:2 (Winter 1974-75), 13.
   4. *Ibid.*
   5. The second time we see the space above the bed the portraits are missing. Is it simply an inconsistency in setting, or are we to draw the obvious implication that not even ideological parents ought to intrude upon the act of love?
   6. Norma McLain Stoop, "Lina Wertmüller and Giancarlo Giannini: Cinematic Counterpoint," *After Dark* 8:2 (April 1976), 34.
   7. *Ibid.*
   8. Although a song must be heard for full effect, and this one especially against the montage of war footage, the verses of "Oh Yeah" yield meaning in their own disjointed fashion. The full text of the song follows (a virgule replaces the refrain "Oh yeah!"): "The ones who don't enjoy themselves even when they

laugh/the ones who worship the corporate image not knowing that they work for someone else/the ones who should have been shot in the cradle . . . Pow!/the ones who say follow me to success but kill me if I fail, so to speak/the ones who say we Italians are the greatest he-men on earth/the ones who are noble Romans/the ones who vote for the right because they are fed up with strikes/the ones who vote white in order not to get dirty/the ones who never get involved with politics/the ones who say be calm, be calm/the ones who still support the king/the ones who say, Oh yeah/the ones who make love standing in their boots and imagine they're in a luxurious bed/the ones who believe Christ is Santa Claus as a young man/the ones who were there/the ones who believe in everything, even in God/the ones who sing the national anthem/the ones who love their country/the ones who keep going, keep going, just to see how it all ends/the ones who are in garbage up to here/the ones who sleep soundly even with cancer/the ones who even now don't know that the world is round/the ones who are afraid of flying, the ones who have never had a fatal accident, the ones who have had one/the ones who at a certain point in their lives crave the secret weapon—Christ/the ones who are always standing at the bar, the ones who are always in Switzerland/the ones who started early, haven't arrived, and doubt not they're not going to/the ones who lose wars by the skin of their teeth/the ones who say everything is wrong here/the ones who say never throw away a good laugh/now let's all have a good laugh, Oh yeah, Oh yeah, Oh yeah."

9. The story of the film is reported to have been basically the true experience of an extra in the cast of *The Seduction of Mimi*. John Simon, "Wertmüller's 'Seven Beauties'—Call It a Masterpiece," *New York* 9:5 (February 2, 1976), 31.

10. In Naples it is a common sight to see housewives letting down baskets from their windows.

11. Simon, "Wertmüller's 'Seven Beauties,'" 30.

12. Molly Haskell, "Lina Wertmüller Is a Radical Chick with an Eye for the Rooster," *The Village Voice* (January 26, 1976), 12.

13. Pauline Kael, "Seven Fatties," *The New Yorker* 51 (February 16, 1976), 107.

14. Simon, "Wertmüller's 'Seven Beauties,'" 28.

15. *Ibid.*

16. *Ibid.*

17. Kael, "Seven Fatties," 109.

18. Bruno Bettelheim, "Surviving," *The New Yorker* 52:24 (August 2, 1976), 50.

CONCLUSION: AN IMAGE OF THE FUTURE

1. Bruno Bettelheim, "Surviving," *The New Yorker* 52:24 (August 2, 1976), 31-52.

2. Terrence Des Pres, "Bleak Comedies: Lina Wertmüller's Artful Method," *Harper's* 252 (June 1976), 26-28.

3. Rene Wellek and Austin Warren, *Theory of Literature*, 3rd ed. (New York: Harcourt, Brace & World, 1962), p. 156.

4. Bettelheim, "Surviving," 31.

5. *Ibid.*

6. *Ibid*, p. 36.

7. Terrence Des Pres as quoted in Bettelheim, "Surviving," 36.

Notes

8. *Ibid.*
9. *Ibid.*
10. *Ibid.*, p. 47.
11. *Ibid.*, p. 52.
12. Des Pres, "Bleak Comedies," 26.
13. *Ibid.*
14. *Ibid.*
15. *Ibid.*, p. 28.
16. *Ibid.*, p. 27
17. Luigi Barzini, *The Italians* (New York: Bantam Books, Inc., 1965), Chapter 8, pp. 139 ff.
18. As quoted in Barzini, *The Italians,* p. 153.
19. *Ibid.*, p. 152.
20. Gina Blumenfeld seems to understand Wertmüller perfectly when she writes: "What the Anarchist calls for, in his description of the 'New Man,' the 'Man in Disorder,' who must be created to overcome the deadly encroaching order of totalitarianism, is a kind of human solidarity based not on enforced uniformity but on tolerance and appreciation of human diversity. Without this new kind of civilized 'disorder,' humanity is doomed to play out the tragedy foreshadowed by the experience of the camps." "The (Next to) Last Word on Lina Wertmüller," *Cineaste* 7:2 (Spring 1976), 23.
21. In an interview with Paul McIsaac and Gina Blumenfeld, she expresses it this way: "It seems to me that we must remember above all that we are all human beings, that we should not use characteristics which differentiate us to take advantage of other human beings. The social harmony which we seek must be based on diversity, on creative disorder, on a multiplicity of people and opinions." "You Cannot Make the Revolution on Film: An Interview with Lina Wertmüller," *Cineaste* 7:2 (Spring 1976), 8.

INTERVIEW WITH LINA WERTMULLER

1. As it turned out, the film of Gore Vidal's Caligula did not, according to him, follow his original script anyway. He told Navone and me that his Caligula was a man obsessed with death. His Caligula would watch people die as if to discover what secrets death might hold.
2. The Jesuit in *The Magic Mountain* is an ambiguous character, to say the least. Naphta is a Jew turned Jesuit but not quite. He is not, as the young hero of the book (Hans Castorp) puts it, a "proper" Jesuit, having never been ordained or taken final vows. What Castorp (and apparently Thomas Mann) imagines a Jesuit to be is only a little less strange that Naphta's own misapprehension. The conversation between Naphta and Settembrini (Castorp's Virgil on the Magic Mountain) that Lina Wertmüller has reference to is probably that section of Chapter VI entitled "The City of God, and Deliverance by Evil" in which Naphta speaks of the proletariat taking up the task of Pope Gregory the Great "to strike terror into the world for the healing of the world, that man may finally achieve salvation and deliverance, and win back at length to freedom from law and destruction of classes, to his original status as child of God" (from H.T. Lowe-Porter's translation of *The Magic Mountain* published by Penguin Books, 1960, p. 404).
3. No doubt Ms. Wertmüller intends this remark with a certain irony. Actu-

ally, we were unable to find any such council on record, and while certain theologians have questioned the quality of a woman's soul, the official teaching of the Church—much to our relief—has always been that at least she had one.

4. In Paraguay the State stepped in and undid all the work of the Jesuits among the Indians; in China the Church stepped in and undid their work among the Chinese. Both chapters in the history of cultural interaction make highly instructive reading.

5. It is interesting to note that Wertmüller rejects this concept of God because, like Caligula, he sets traps for men.

6. The passage Wertmüller has reference to is probably from the same Chapter VI. "Whatever profits man," Naphta begins, "that is the truth" (*Ibid.*, p. 404).

7. Guido Ceronetti, *La carta è stanca* (Milano: Adelphi Edizioni, 1976), pp. 386, 387.

Index

Allen, Tom, 13
All Screwed Up, 5, 15, 22–24, 27–29, 44
All the President's Men, 13
Altman, Robert, 12
Amelia, Lucio, 60
Antonioni, Michelangelo, 4, 41
Arrupe, Pedro, 82
Ashby, Hal, 12

Balcony, The, 21
Barzini, Luigi, 19, 37, 74
Basilischi, I, 10, 38
Bazin, René, 14
Belli, Agostina, 47
Bergen, Candice, 98
Bergman, Ingmar, 4
Bertolucci, Bernardo, 14
Bettelheim, Bruno, 66, 69–72
Betti, Ugo, 33
Bignamini, Nino, 23
Biskind, Peter, 47
Blumenfeld, Gina, 26
Boheme, La, 39
Bronzino, Angelo, 64

Caligula, 76–78
Canby, Vincent, 14
Carta è stanca, La, 86
Cavani, Liliana, 13
Ceronetti, Guido, 85–86
Chaplin, Charles, 11
Conti, Mario, 56
Costa-Gavras, 11
Crossan, John Dominic, 3, 73, 74

Dali, Salvador, 22
Danieli, Isa, 22
Dante Alighieri, 22, 57, 64
de Chirico, Giorgio, 42
de Felice, Ermelinad, 60
de Filippo, Eduardo, 13
de Sica, Vittorio, 14, 41
delli Colli, Tonino, 60
Des Pres, Terrence, 69, 72–73
Diberti, Luigi, 22
di Orio, Piero, 54
Dostoevsky, Feodor, 80, 85

Eisenstein, Sergei, 14, 22–23
Eli, 46
Engels, Friedrich, 49

Fellini, Federico, 4, 10, 13, 14
Fiore, Elena, 50, 55
Frankl, Victor, 69
Fugitive, The, 33

Genesis, The Book of, 2, 19
Genet, Jean, 21
Gerard, Lillian, 12
Giannini, Giancarlo, 10, 31, 36, 47, 54, 74, 98
Gilliatt, Penelope, 12
Golding, William, 34
Goldoni, Carlo, 26
Gregory the Great, 101
Guevara, Che, 48
Guccione, Bob, 76

Haskell, Molly, 14, 26, 62
Herlitzka, Roberto, 61
Hitler, Adolf, 54, 58, 63, 77

Iannaci, Enzo, 56, 65
Ieri, oggi, domani, 41
Inferno, 50, 58

Jacobs, Diane, 12
Jesus Christ, 3–4, 63, 67, 80
Job, Enrico, 10, 14, 60

Kael, Pauline, 13, 63, 66
Kennedy, John F., 1
Ketcham, Charles B., 2
King, Martin Luther, 1
Koch, Ilse, 58
Kosinsky, Jerzy, 69, 72

Lear, Norman, 13
Lee, Margaret, 40
Lefebvre, Archbishop Marcel, 83
Lenin, Nikolai, 49
Let's Talk About Men, 5, 26, 38–42, 52
Lizards, The, 10, 38
Lord of the Flies, 34
Love and Anarchy, 5, 15, 21, 24, 26, 35–36, 42–44, 74, 81

Magic Mountain, The, 78, 85
Malatesta, Enrico, 43
Mancini, Giacomo, 11
Manfredi, Nino, 38
Mann, Thomas, 78, 85

INDEX

Man's Search for Meaning, 69
Mao Tse-tung, 48
Marciano, Francesca, 56
Marx, Karl, 45, 48
Mastroiani, Flora, 10
McIsaac, Paul, 26
Melato, Mariangela, 31, 35, 48
Mimi, Metalworker Wounded in Honor, 46
Mussolini, Benito, 21, 42, 43, 54, 60, 61, 73–74

Nashville, 12
Navone, John, 76
Night Full of Rain, A, 98

Ojetti, Ugo, 74

Pakula, Alan, 12
Palmi, Doriglia, 62
Pagni, Eros, 43
Paluzzi, Luciana, 38
Pasolini, Pier Paolo, 14
Polito, Lina, 22, 35
Porter, Carolyn, 34
Purgatorio, 22

Quacinella, Lucy, 11, 12

Rapisarda, Sara, 22
Red Desert, 41
Renoir, Jean, 4
Revelation, The Book of, 25, 53
Rey, Fernando, 58
Ricci, Matteo, 83
Richard II, 19
"Ride of the Valkyries, The," 57
Riley, Brooks, 12, 13
Rita the Mosquito, 10

St. Francis of Assisi, 80
St. Ignatius Loyola, 24, 82
St. Jude, 39
St. Paul, 35, 45, 79
Samuel, 46

Seduction of Mimi, The, 5, 10, 11, 19–20, 24, 29, 30, 35, 36–37, 44, 46–52, 81
Seven Beauties, 5, 12, 13, 21–22, 24, 29–30, 42, 52–68, 69–72, 74, 80
Shakespeare, William, 19
Shampoo, 12
Signorelli, Maria, 9
Simon, John, 4, 11, 13, 14, 26, 60, 66, 76
Soleri, Paulo, 24
Spiritual Exercises, The, 24
Stoler, Shirley, 29, 58
Strike, 22, 23
Strong Are Lonely, The, 83
"Surviving," 69–72
Survivor, The, 69
Swept Away, 5, 11, 13, 20–21, 24, 29, 30–35, 44–46, 52, 81

Teilhard de Chardin, Pierre, 33
Thomas, Paul, 34
Träume, 57
Traviata, La, 49
Two and Two Are No Longer Four, 10

"Venus, Cupid, Folly, and Time," 64
Vidal, Gore, 76
Visconti, Luchino, 13, 14
Vitale, Enzo, 56
Volontè, Claudio, 22
Von Ranke, Leopold, 84
Vukotic, Milena, 39

Wagner, Richard, 57
Warren, Austin, 70
Wellek, Rene, 70
Wertmüller von Elgg, Erich, 8
Wilder, Amos, 2
Willis, Ellen, 26
Wood, Michael, 13, 14, 27, 29

Zeffirelli, Franco, 10, 39